Chilson's History of Fort Sisseton

by Norma Johnson

Norma Johnson
Ft. Sisseton

First Edition

Printed by State Publishing & Printing
303 East Sioux, Pierre, South Dakota 57501

ISBN 0-9652144-0-0 (Paperback)
ISBN 0-9652144-1-9 (Hardcover)

Library of Congress Catalog Card number:
96-85698

Cover photo by John Front

Dedicated
to the memory
of

Herman P. Chilson
(1905-1986)

ACKNOWLEDGMENTS

A sincere thanks to the Chilson family for entrusting me with all the research materials; to Wendy Lewis, naturalist, South Dakota Department of Game, Fish & Parks, Roy Lake State Park, for her assistance and advice; and to Maryann L. Joyner, curatorial assistant at the Norman Rockwell Museum at Stockbridge.

Norma Johnson

PREFACE

Herman Chilson's love of history and particularly that of the northeastern section of South Dakota was well known to his friends, family and fellow historians. He spent considerable time researching and gathering the history of Fort Sisseton (Wadsworth) with the intention of someday writing a book. That day did not come. Herman passed away in 1986. His files and boxes of notes, information, books and photos gathered throughout the years were temporarily shelved.

I have attempted to compile this information into a book, hopefully the way Herman would have done. Notes he had underlined and items that he checked off were researched further.

Herman wanted a book that could be shared with all, young and old, a book that would show his love of the history of Fort Sisseton. I trust I have conveyed that feeling.

Norma Johnson

TABLE OF CONTENTS

Page No.

Chapter One

Westward to Dakota Territory

". . . I have today located Fort Wadsworth."
Major John Clowney
August 1, 1864

The sun on those brisk October mornings made the marching more bearable for the frontier soldiers during one of their rare morning dress parades. Fall was in the air and the blue wool uniforms felt good, but as one soldier uttered, "Not yet comfortable." These soldiers, members of Company E, Thirtieth Wisconsin Infantry Volunteers, were instrumental in the initial building of Fort Wadsworth, Dakota Territory, in 1864.

Fort Wadsworth received its name in General Order number 197 from the War Department on May 12, 1864. That order described it as situated on the James River. It was named in honor of New York General James W. Wadsworth who was killed in the Battle of the Wilderness in Virginia on April 2, 1864.

The motley assortment of buildings surrounding the soldiers on the parade grounds was in various stages of completion. The blacksmith shop and the two blockhouses of hewn oak were completed while the hospital, quartermaster's and commissary buildings were almost finished. The portable sawmill had been in operation since August 17. Because winter was approaching, temporary log structures and sod huts were hastily erected for the soldiers' use.

There were no towns; this was a fortress on the desolate prairie in eastern Dakota Territory in 1864. Fort Wadsworth was situated on the western edge of the Coteau des Prairies (French for "Hills of the Prairies") and nestled on a piece of land surrounded by a chain of lakes known as Kettle Lakes. At that time, the road to the post was through water and over a land bar connecting two of the lakes.

To understand why a fort was built so far from civilization, one must recall the history that led up to its establishment.

The Civil War had divided the young country. The United States, under President Abraham Lincoln, was engrossed in keeping the nation together. Emigrant trains were moving westward, lured by free tracts of land in the Midwest. Others headed westward to find their fortunes in the gold fields in Idaho.

In the neighboring state of Minnesota, the Sioux Indians were dissatisfied with their living conditions. As a result of the Treaties of 1851 and 1858, these Indians exchanged title to twenty-eight million acres of land for yearly annuity payments and a narrow reserve of land along the south side of the Minnesota River. Seven thousand Indians occupied the seventy by twenty mile strip of land. In the northern part, the Sisseton and Wahpetons occupied the Upper Sioux Agency (Yellow Medicine), which included their old village sites. Thirty miles to the south, the Mdewakantonwans and the Wahpekutes lived in the Lower Agency (Redwood). One agent supervised the business affairs of both agencies.

The treaties also contained provisions to encourage the Indians to become farmers. However, most of them remained 'blanket Indians' and continued to hunt and fish. The 'farmer Indians', dressed in white man's clothing, lived in houses and tried to raise crops. The crop failure in 1861 almost led to starvation in 1862; moreover, the promised food rations and annuity payments from the United States government were late in coming.

The late arrival of monies was because Congress was slow in appropriating funds. When the funds were finally appropriated, the United States Treasury Department spent a month deciding whether to pay in paper currency or in gold. Five thousand Indians gathered at the Upper Sioux Agency on July 14,

MAP OF THE
SIOUX OUTBREAK AND WAR
IN SOUTHWESTERN MINNESOTA
1862

Scale of Miles

County Boundaries
Reservations with dates
Dakota or Sioux
Ojibway or Chippewa
Winnebago

Minnesota Historical Society

3

1862. The government warehouse was filled with food, but Agent Thomas J. Galbraith wanted to wait and hand out food when the annuity payment arrived. Then on August 4, five hundred Indians surrounded the warehouse and removed sacks of flour. Captain John F. Marsh of Company B, 56th Minnesota Infantry, and Lieutenant Timothy J. Sheehan of Company C, 5th Regiment, Minnesota Infantry, who were there with some soldiers, both urged Agent Galbraith to issue more pork, flour and annuity goods. Agent Galbraith refused.

During this time, some Indians resorted to hunting trips to their old hunting ground; others demanded food or goods when they stopped at white people's cabins.

The 'blanket Indians,' along with the medicine men and warriors who opposed farming, planned an attack on the 'farmer Indians' living in the Yellow Medicine River area. Many thought this was a good time because so many of the white men were sent to fight in the Civil War. Minnesota had even recruited a company of half-breed volunteers called the Renville Rangers from the Upper Indian Agency near Granite Falls. The Indians thought the state was hard up for men and especially vulnerable. However, an incident in Acton Township, Meeker County (west of present-day Grove City, Minnesota) changed their plans.

Sunday, August 17, 1862, four Indian men (Brown Wing, Killing Ghost, Runs Against When Crawling, and Breaking Up) from the Rice Creek band of the Sioux, were hunting in Acton Woods. They stopped at Robinson Jones' Trading Post and asked for whiskey, but were refused. They argued and then left. When one of the men picked up some chicken eggs along a fence line, his friend reminded him that the eggs belonged to a white man. He promptly smashed the eggs and swore to kill the first white man he saw. They soon came to the Howard Baker cabin where the Robinson Jones and Viranus Webster families were outside visiting. The Indian men stopped and carried on a conversation with them, and the talk about guns led to a trade. Howard Baker traded his gun to one of the men for $3.00 "to boot". They agreed to have a target match. The Indians fired first, then reloaded their guns. The white men fired and did not reload. The four Indians then turned on them and killed Howard Baker, Mr. and Mrs. Robinson Jones and Viranus Webster. Mrs. Baker fled to the safety of the house. The Indians ran. When they came to the Jones Trading Post they shot Clara Wilson (Robinson Jones' niece) who was standing in the doorway.

The Indian who swore to kill the first white man he saw kept his word.

The men stole a team of horses and buckboard from the nearby A. M. Ecklund farm and fled to their village at Rice Creek. They bragged about what they had done, and their people took them to Traveling Hail, the tribe's speaker. He sent word to all leaders to attend a midnight council at Little Crow's house. Little Crow had adopted white man's ways but was still the hereditary chief of his tribe.

The leaders of the Wahpekutes and the Mdewakantons from the Lower Sioux Agency arrived for the council. The leaders of the Upper Sioux Agency, Standing Buffalo, Scarlet Plume and Wanaton, could not attend since they were buffalo hunting along the Sheyenne River up north. A Wahpeton runner informed the Sissetons of the egg incident and the council meeting. The Sissetons held their council and informed their men not to get involved. At first, Little Crow opposed going to war; but when the leaders threatened him, he reversed his decision and offered to be their leader. Plans were made to attack the trading post at Lower Agency at daybreak.

During the next thirty-eight days of August and September, several battles and skirmishes took place in what is now known as the Minnesota Uprising of 1862. After the Battle of Wood Lake and the death of Chief Mankato, the Indians surrendered their captives at Camp Release (now Montevideo, Minnesota). More than 700 white settlers lost their lives as the result of this uprising that lasted less than six weeks.

Little Crow and about 150 followers fled into Canada hoping to obtain help from the British government in exchange for the help they had given the British in the War of 1812. Many Sioux fled into Dakota Territory. Although some of their young men had joined in the fighting, many of the Sisseton-Wahpetons did not leave, since they had been officially neutral.

General Henry H. Sibley's committee of five officers conducted a court martial of 302 Indians. The guilty In-

Little Crow, a Sioux chief and leader of the Minnesota Uprising of 1862.
Minnesota Historical Society.

General Henry R. Sibley. General Sibley was an agent for the American Fur Company. He spoke the Sioux language. The Indians gave him two names, Wah-ze-o-mannee (Walker in the Pines) and Wah-Pe-Ton-Hauska (The Tall Trader). He served as Minnesota's first governor from 1858-1860.
Minnesota Historical Society.

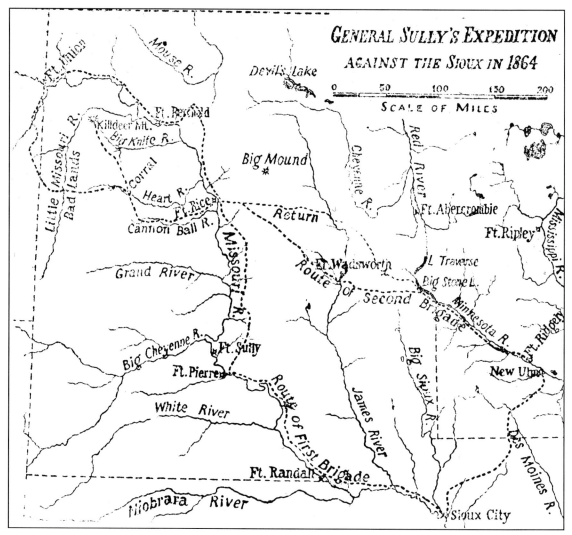

GENERAL SULLY'S EXPEDITION AGAINST THE SIOUX IN 1864

SCALE OF MILES

General Sully's Expedition.

Minnesota Historical Society.

dians were sent to Camp Lincoln near Fort Snelling, Minnesota. President Lincoln reviewed their records, and thirty-eight Indians were hanged in Mankato, Minnesota, on December 26, 1862.

The $71,000 in gold coins the Indians were to receive as annuity payments arrived the day the Lower Agency was attacked, August 18, 1862.

Major General John Pope, Commander of the Headquarters Department of the Northwest, ordered two columns of soldiers to march into Dakota Territory to capture the hostiles. General Sully and his troops traveled up the Mis-

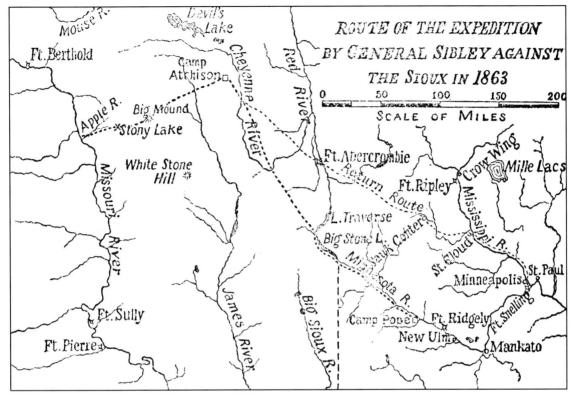

General Sibley's Expedition.

Minnesota Historical Society.

souri River, and General Sibley's infantry marched northwest from Fort Ridgely, Minnesota, into Dakota Territory towards Devils Lake where he was to meet General Sully's cavalry. Their combined goal was to capture or destroy the Sioux warriors involved in the Minnesota Uprising.

General Sibley's 3,300 soldiers, 65 scouts, 300 wagons and over 3,500 mules, horses and cattle spread out for six miles. This was the largest military expedition under one command in this area. Because of the drought conditions the previous two years and the extremely hot weather, the marching often began at 4 a.m. and ended around noon. The Indian scouts took the lead five miles ahead of the column and patrolled an area three to ten miles in width on both sides of the column. Major Joseph R. Brown was Chief of Scouts on this expedition.

As soon as Minnesota Governor Alexander Ramsey heard of the uprising, he began organizing an army, placing them under the command of General H. H. Sibley. Major General John Pope, Commander of the Department of the

Northwest, suggested a series of army posts be built in Dakota Territory to prevent further hostilities. One post was to be built at Devils Lake (Fort Hayes), one on the Yellowstone River (Fort Stevenson), one near Fort Clark (Fort Rice), and one on the James River (Fort Wadsworth). These four forts were needed to prevent attacks on the Minnesota frontier, to provide protection for the settlers entering the area, and to provide protection for the would-be-miners enroute to the gold fields in Idaho. There was also a potential need to protect the 'farmer Indians' from the 'blanket Indians'.

On October 7, 1862, Dakota Territory's Governor and Commander-in-chief of the Militia, Dr. William Jayne, sent the following special order to the headquarters of the Dakota Militia in Yankton, Dakota Territory:

> I have concluded to accept eight companies of volunteer militia (four companies of infantry and four companies of cavalry) to serve nine months unless sooner discharged. This force will be tendered to Major General Pope for his acceptance into the United States service for the said term of nine months. The officers and men of the cavalry companies will be required to furnish their own horses, equipment and clothing until such time as the army can be otherwise furnished. Rations will be furnished the men as soon as allowed to similar companies in the United States service.

Major Joseph R. Brown was the first Chief of Scouts at Fort Wadsworth and served as special military agent at Fort Wadsworth. He also had a sub-contract to carry mail between Redwood Falls, MN, and Fort Wadsworth and owned the stageline from Redwood Falls to Wadsworth and Fort Ridgely, MN.

Chilson Photo Collection.

General Sibley was charged with the establishment of the Devils Lake and the James River posts. However, in May 1864, Edward M. Stanton, Secretary of War, ordered the Sixth Minnesota Volunteers to go to Arkansas and Louisiana; thus, the post at Devils Lake was never established.

A detachment of four companies of infantry left Fort Ridgely, Minnesota, to start the construction of Fort Wadsworth on the James River near present-day Aberdeen, South Dakota. However, due to the lack of timber and on the advice of Pierre Bottineau and Norman Kittson (scouts and fur traders) and Major Joseph R. Brown (Chief of Scouts during the Sibley Expedition), the fort would be established further east, near the Kettle Lakes. A temporary post was to be established on the James River.

Major John Clowney and three companies of the Thirtieth Wisconsin Volunteers were dispatched to the proposed site in the Coteau Hills on June 11, 1864.

These companies of infantry volunteers were temporarily assigned to construct Fort Wadsworth. Enlisted men were employed as mechanics, woodcutters, common laborers and quarrymen. Officers worked as foremen and engineers.

Before Fort Wadsworth was actually established, a detachment of soldiers escorted Captain Fisk and his wagon train of emigrants (146 men, 7 women, a dozen children and 96 teams). This party was scheduled to leave Fort Ridgely, Minnesota, around July 1, 1864. Fisk planned to go past the proposed site of Fort Wadsworth and thus requested military escort. General Sibley had written in return that the wagon train could travel with the army detachment enroute to construct the fort. However, if they wanted further assistance, it would be up to Major Clowney to order a spare detachment of cavalry to escort the Fisk train to the Grand River. Unfortunately, Captain James Fisk's wagon train arrived at Fort Ridgely on July 13, three days after the soldiers had left for Fort Wadsworth. Consequently, after the wagon train's departure, Lieutenant Henry F. Phillips and fifty soldiers from Company 1, Second Minnesota cavalry, were sent to overtake and escort the wagon train to the site of the proposed fort.

Major Clowney's report on the last two weeks of the journey to the Kettle Lakes Camp No. 18 reveals some of the hardships they encountered on that hot, dusty journey.

Headquarters Garrison for Fort Wadsworth
Camp No. 18 on Kettle Lake
August 1, 1864

Captain R. C. Olin,
Assistant Adjutant-General

Sir:

In continuation of my report, I have the honor to submit the following:

July 16, marched from camp No. 7 on Inkpah River at 5:30 a.m. a north-westerly direction, camping at 2 p.m. on a small lake or slough, called by some Lake Ramsey. Bad water, no wood, grass in abundance. Distance from Camp No. 7 - eleven miles.

July 17, left camp No. 8 at 3:15 a.m. Traveled in a northwesterly direction about fourteen miles, camping on a small lake of bad water at 2 p.m.

9

Passed some dried up lakes on the road. No wood near camping grounds; good grazing; hot day. Four oxen died on the road from the heat.

July 18, marched from camp No. 9 at 7:30 a.m. in same direction as yesterday. Camped on Yellow Earth Creek at 10 a.m. Good water, wood and grass. Distance of march-four miles. Weather was too hot to render it safe to drive the cattle to the next camping ground.

July 19, left camp No. 10 at 4 a.m. Marched northwest about fourteen miles, camping on a small creek at 12 p.m. Plenty of water and grass. Wood enough for camping purposes.

July 20, left camp No. 11 at 4:30 a.m. Marched northwest about ten miles to water; rested at 9 a.m. about two hours; turned out the stock to graze. Camped on Bullhead Lake at 1:30 p.m. Wood scarce; grass plenty. Distance marched this day sixteen miles.

July 21, resumed the march at 4 a.m. Traveled almost due north about twelve miles, when the road inclined to the west. Passed some small lakes. Camped at 10 a.m. near Saint Peter's River, between Big Stone Lake and Lake Traverse. Plenty of wood and grass. Distance marched to-day about sixteen miles. Gabriel Renville visited my camp and gave information with regard to the route across and to the head of the Coteau.

July 22, left camp No. 13 on Saint Peter's River at 4 a.m. Marched almost due west toward the Coteau. Made crossing over a branch of Saint Peter's River about four miles from last camp. Camped on small stream at 10 a.m. on the side of the Coteau. Distance marched to-day ten miles.

July 23, left camp No. 14 at 4 a.m. Marched in a westerly direction over the Coteau; country very rolling; passed a number of small lakes; camped a 12m (miles) on a lake about four miles long and over a half mile wide, named by the Indians Enemy Sinus [Swim] Lake; an abundance of fish; plenty of wood, water and grass. Distance traveled to-day twelve miles.

July 24, left camp No. 15 at 4 a.m. Traveled north-northwest over rolling country on the Coteau; passed a number of small lakes; road rather rocky; camped at 2 p.m. on small lake; plenty of wood and grass. Distance marched seventeen miles.

July 25, left camp No. 16 at 6 a.m. Marched in same direction as yesterday; camped at 9 a.m. on south side of a lake of a circular form, called by scouts Kettle Lake.

July 26, remained in camp. Sent detachment of infantry, cavalry and one piece of artillery to explore the country on James River from the mouth of the Elm River to the mouth of the Bone Hill River, under command of Captain L. S. Burton, Thirtieth Wisconsin Volunteers.

July 27, command remained in camp.

July 28, moved one mile to a pleasant land commanding point; staked out and went into permanent camp to await the return of detachment sent to examine the country on James River between the mouth of Elm River and Bone Hill River. Throughout my entire route from Fort Ridgely here, I have been fortunate in obtaining good camps, which, by throwing up a few rifle-pits, rendered them easy to defend in the event of an attack. None of my scouts have up to this date reported the presence of any hostile Indians.

John Clowney, Major
Thirtieth Regiment, Wisconsin
Infantry, Commanding

Captain James Fisk penned this account the day Lieutenant Phillips brought his wagon train into the Kettle Lakes camp.

The Fisk Expedition to the gold fields in Idaho waiting for the military escort from Fort Wadsworth
South Dakota Game, Fish & Parks

July 30, Reached that magnificent cluster of Lakes known as Kettle [Fort] Lakes, so graphically described by [Joseph N.] Nicollet. Here we found the Camp of the expedition that had been sent out from Fort Snelling to locate and build a Post somewhere near or on the James River, on the proposed line of travel, to be called Fort Wadsworth, in honor I suppose of the brave and lamented General [James S. Wadsworth] of that name. I soon had a visit from Officers and men of the camp, many of whom I was acquainted with. I was told that they had halted there and sent forward a reconnoitering party to the James River, who were hourly expected back, with a report whether the site they were on, or some other on the James River, which is about 40 miles west, would be selected for the post. The party returned next morning just as we were moveing on, and reported unfavorable for the James, so Fort Wadsworth is being built amidst those blue, oak skirted lakes, well upon the Coteau De Prairie, surrounded on three sides by water, glorious prairies stretching away in every direction, stocked with game of evry description, and on the route which must, of all other, be established from the western border to Montana and the Pacific side. I received several favors from the party and for courtesies extended by all officers of the command, I am their debtor.
National Archives, File 63F, NARG 94

The next day, Lieutenant Phillips and a detachment of soldiers escorted the Fisk wagon train to the Missouri River, returning to Fort Wadsworth August 27.

On August 1, 1864, Major Clowney made the following statement:

I would respectfully state that the point I have selected for the fort has no disadvantages that cannot be obtained in any other place. The old grass not having been burned off, will make it troublesome to obtain the amount of hay needed; but another year, by attending to having the hay ground burned, there will be little trouble. There is timber sufficient for building purposes, and fuel in abundance, with good water, with clay for brick, and limestone. The site is the strongest without improvement I have seen and the country around the head of the Coteau is far ahead of my expectations. I have today located Fort Wadsworth . . .

Chapter Two

Scouts and Scout Camps

" You told me to pick out reliable men. I have done so. . . "
Gabriel Renville
February 1863

The use of Indians as scouts had proved beneficial during the Minnesota Uprising and during General Sibley's 1863 Military Expedition. In February 1863, Gabriel Renville went to General Sibley and suggested that mixed bloods and fullbloods be picked as scouts. Besides himself, he suggested the names of Michael Renville, Daniel Renville, Issac Renville, John Moore, Thomas Robertson, and four fullbloods: Two Stars, Echat-tu ke-ya, Eneehah and Wah-su-ho-wastay.

When laughed at for suggesting fullblood Indians, Gabriel replied, "You told me to pick out reliable men. I have done so. There are fullblood Indians who are more steadfast, more dependable than mixed bloods. That is why I have chosen them."

Their names were approved by Washington, D.C. Alex LaFramboise and Joseph LaFramboise went to the Rice Creek Camp and were added as scouts by General Sibley. They were sent out on their own as scouts in February 1863 and later on were with General Sibley. Two Stars, Joseph Leblanc, Antoine Renville, Hanyokeyan, Ahwetanenah, Maahpeyahwahkoonzay, Wahhahchankah were scouts at Fort Ridgely.

With the establishment of Fort Wadsworth, scouts assisted the soldiers in capturing hostile Indians and brought in the surrendered Indians. Scout camps were established in strategic places close to the Indian trails in Dakota Territory and along both sides of the Minnesota border. Each camp was manned by ten or fifteen scouts and their families. Some of these twenty or so scout camps were more important and better fortified than others.

General Sibley gave orders on how to choose and prepare a scout camp. The sites were to be easy to defend, preferably on high points of land far from trees and ravines. The site was to be square with artillery placed at opposite angles so that all approaches could be covered with gunfire. Rifle pits were to be dug every night.

To clear up the misunderstanding about the term "Chief of Scouts", there was a chief of scouts at each scout camp as well as a Chief of Scouts overseeing all the established scout camps. Major Joseph R. Brown was appointed the first Chief of Scouts on October 14, 1863. He held this position until August 9, 1864, when he was then appointed Special Military Agent at Fort Wadsworth. Pierre Bottineau became the second Chief of Scouts on August 10, 1864, followed by Gabriel Renville on May 1, 1865.

Pay for the Chief of Scouts and others varied from time to time. On February 15, 1866, the wages for the chiefs of the scouting stations had been raised from $30 to $40 per month. Chief of Scouts Gabriel Renville's pay was raised to $3.50 per day while Sam Brown, the interpreter, was paid $2.00 per day. A regular scout was paid $1.00 a day, plus fifty cents per day for each horse, plus rations for himself and each member of his family. Rations included pork, beef, flour or bread, coffee or tea, sugar, soap and salt, and were issued every ten days. Children under ten years of age received half rations.

By 1865, scout camps were operating at full capacity. On October 21, 1865, General Sibley ordered Major Brown, Special Military Agent at Fort Wadsworth, to form a scouting force to drive the hostile Indians west of the James River and keep them there. The scouting force was staffed by fullblood and mixed-blood Indians who had sworn allegiance to the United States. Their orders were simple: "When meeting hostiles, take no prisoners." The scouts were to assist in controlling the hostile bands of Indians and to patrol the area. Scouts without horses put up hay and guarded Fort Wadsworth and the Scout Headquarters, east of the fort.

In June 1866, Congress passed a law legalizing the enlistment of one thousand scouts. However, it took the army almost a year to implement the law.

Commander Hayman at Fort Wadsworth was ordered to enlist fifty scouts. They were required to enlist for five years and receive the same pay, rations and clothing as regular soldiers. Since Fort Wadsworth was considered the most important post, it was designated as the training center for the eastern half of Dakota Territory. Of the fifty scouts trained, fifteen were assigned to Fort Ransom, fifteen to Fort Abercrombie and twenty to Fort Wadsworth.

The scout camps are grouped here according to location. Not all camps were in operation at the same time. The Fort Wadsworth Cluster Scout Camps included Military Agency, Vasseur, Surrendered, Dry Wood Lake, Hay Meadow and Lake Traverse. The Central Scout Camps consisted of Big Island, Buzzard's Roost, Drifting Guts, Kampeska and Wabé. Listed in the Northern Scout Camps were Bears Den, Head of Coteau, Maple River, Sheyenne River, Skunk Lake and Twin Lakes. James River Scout Camps included Bone Hill, Elm River, James River, Oak Grove, Mocassin River and Snake Creek.

Fort Wadsworth Cluster Scout Camps

Military Agency

The Military Agency Scout Camp was set up on the shore of the Kettle Lakes, one mile east of Fort Wadsworth. It was often referred to as Agency, Akipa's Camp or Fort Wadsworth Agency. The Indians named it Cegaiyeapi meaning "Where They Found the Kettle". Nineteen-year-old Sam Brown was chief of scouts here and at Vasseur Camp in 1864. One of Sam's duties was issuing rations to the Indian scouts and their families every ten days. These rations were supplied by Fort Wadsworth's commissary officer. It took Sam a day and a half to complete the task.

The Military Agency was the headquarters or command post for all Indian business and scouting operations. This was also the home of Major Joseph Brown and his family. The scouts stationed here were employed year-round. These scouts carried mail and military orders, usually traveling in small groups of two or four. According to Sam Brown's diary the scouts set up their camp, about fifty lodges, on a little hill opposite the Military Agency building.

Major Brown supervised the construction of the Military Headquarters building, a two-story, eight-room log house. This was the first known shingled-roof house in what is now northeastern South Dakota. The house was en-

SENTINELS FOR THE FORT

The Indian scouts were devoted to duty, and when given the order, "When meeting hostiles, take no prisoners," they loyally obeyed. Twenty scouts camps were scattered across eastern South Dakota, along the James River and as far south as Oakwood Lakes. Because of this strategic location of scout camps and because of the work of the scouts, Fort Sisseton never came under attack.

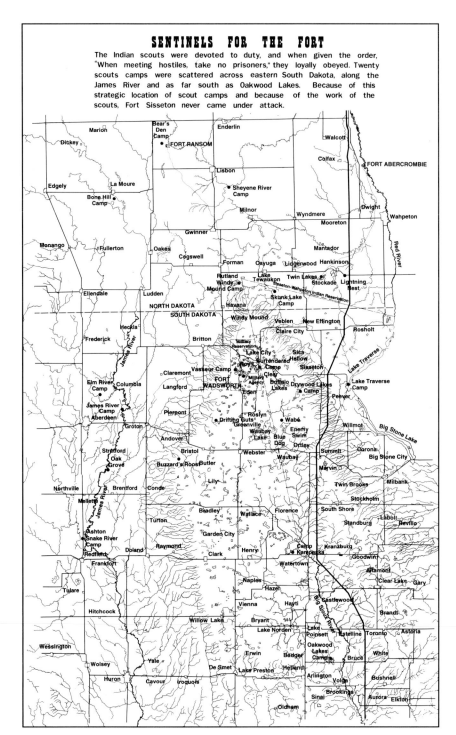

Fort Wadsworth Scout Camp map.

By Herman Chilson and Dave Johnson.
South Dakota Game, Fish & Parks

closed within a one hundred feet square stockade made of twelve-foot bur oak posts with sharp points on top. There were portholes for muskets and four blockhouses built, one in each corner of the stockade.

**This old log house was the scouts' headquarters, located east of the fort.
Today it is in Browns Valley, MN.**

Chilson Photo Collection.

Major Brown was appointed Special Military Agent at Fort Wadsworth and vicinity on August 9, 1864. As Special Military Agent, Brown reported to the Commander at Fort Wadsworth. General Sibley felt that Major Brown was an experienced person, capable of communicating with the Indians. Brown's appointment allowed Major Clowney to devote more time to the construction of the buildings.

Major Brown set up the rules and regulations for the scout camps subject to the approval of the commanding officer at Fort Wadsworth. He submitted monthly reports and ordered the supplies. On one notable occasion in April, 1866, Major Brown ordered ten thousand dollars of provisions in one order for the surrendered Indians.

At the close of the Indian troubles in 1866, Major Brown purchased the building, dismantled it, carefully marked each piece, stacked the pieces in wagons and transported it all forty miles by oxen to Lac Travers (present-day Browns Valley, Minnesota). After it was rebuilt, it was used as a home, an agency house for the Sisseton Sioux, a stagecoach station, a newspaper office and a post office. In 1871, after the death of Major Brown, it was again torn down, logs marked, and it was moved to the west side of Browns Valley and reassembled. Today, it is the Sam Brown Museum, the only known log building from Fort Wadsworth in existence today.

Vasseur Scout Camp

Vasseur Scout Camp was an extension of the Military Agency. Sam Brown was chief of scouts of both camps. The Vasseur scouts were listed with the Agency scouts. This camp was located three quarters of a mile northeast of Fort Wadsworth. Vasseur Camp was different in many ways from the other scout camps. It was only a quarter mile from neighboring Military Agency, while other camps were fifteen or more miles apart. Vasseur was named for the Vasseur brothers, Louis and Francois, both scouts. Scouts stationed here were white men hired as clerks, mechanics, masons, carpenters, blacksmiths, brickmakers, and wheelwrights. They built and repaired cabins, stockades, and stables and were not required to go out scouting until the last year when only four scouts were hired as scouts and couriers.

Surrendered Camp

Major Brown received permission from General Pope in Milwaukee, Wisconsin, to establish a camp for the surrendered Indians. The Indians at the James River camp did not have enough food and were being taunted by the hostile Indians. Brown set up Surrendered Camp (also known as Sisseton Camp) in March 1865 on Roy Lake (Fish Lake) about five miles northeast of Fort Wadsworth. Majors Brown and Rose selected this site because it was easy to defend and had acres of land to raise crops and vegetables, plenty of wood and an abundance of fish. Scarlet Plume (Red Feather) was placed in charge of Surrendered Camp with four scouts. Scarlet Plume was the Sisseton who risked his life to warn General Sibley that hostile Indians planned to murder him.

About one thousand Indians (130 lodges) from the James River Scout Camp arrived at Fort Wadsworth on April 30, 1865, on their way to Surrendered Camp. This was the headquarters for all surrendered Indians who wanted to stop fighting and return to a reserved piece of land with their fam-

**Surrendered Scout Camp. Some of the camp members posed for
this photo in front of an Indian tepee on Roy Lake.**

W. H. Over, State Museum, Vermillion, SD.

ilies. Later in June, six hundred more Indians (150 lodges) surrendered at Fort Wadsworth. This was far more than was expected. These people needed food and clothes. Major Rose from Fort Wadsworth advised District Headquarters he was going to send some scouts and the surrendered men buffalo hunting twenty miles southwest by Lynn Lake. The two hundred fifty buffalo killed provided meat for the winter. Army rations were issued, as well as seeds and hoes were issued for planting. Half of the group was sent to nearby Buffalo Lake (Buffalo Fish Lake) during 1866. It was at this point that Scarlet Plume (Wa-mdi-u-pi-Du-ta) became chief of scouts at Buffalo Lake and Red Iron (Ma-Za-Sha) became chief of scouts at Surrendered Camp for a short period.

Dry Wood Lake Scout Camp

Dry Wood Lake Scout Camp was set up three fourths mile from the east shore of Dry Wood Lake in present-day Roberts County. The women and children camped close to the shore. Ixakiye (Man That Paints His Mouth Red) was appointed chief of scouts in May 1865. Kangi-du-ta (Red Eagle) was chosen to be a courier to carry mail and orders between Fort Wadsworth and Fort Ridgely, Minnesota. He had to be ready to go twenty-four hours a day as emergencies arose.

On October 21, 1865, Major Brown suggested that Dry Wood Lake, Buzzard's Roost, Drifting Guts and Head of the Coteau scout camps be abandoned, to be replaced with camps at Lake Traverse, Enemy Swim and Lake Benton. However, it is apparent that not all his suggestions were approved because some of the former camps were still in operation in December 1865.

Chief Red Iron (Ma-Za-Sha). Red Iron served as a scout at Fort Wadsworth until 1866. As partial payment for his services, he was given a tract of land near what is today known as Red Iron Lake. He was chief of the Sisseton-Wahpeton Reservation until his death in 1884.

Minnesota Historical Society.

Hay Meadow Scout Camp

Hay Meadow Scout Camp was established in May 1865 on top of a hill in what is today Section 16 in Newport Township, Marshall County. On April 1, 1866, Major Brown recommended one chief and fourteen scouts to be stationed at Hay Meadow. From the top of this hill, one could see the Coteau des Prairies to the east and the James River Valley to the west.

The camp was about one hundred eighty feet by two hundred feet according to Vincent Malm, who used to hay the area. He said the embankment was similar to the one at Fort Wadsworth but not as high. Glen Hanson, who played there as a young boy, remembered the banks' being about two and a half feet high and that the camp was crescent shaped. Malm hired a construction crew to level the remains of the camp in the 1940s so that he could hay the area.

Lake Traverse Scout Camp

The Lake Traverse Scout Camp was established on the south end of Lake Traverse in October 1865. It was located on a high hill one fourth mile southwest from the iron post which marks the eastern boundary of the Sisseton-Wahpeton Indian Reservation. This camp was also known as Lac Travers and Camp Ptan-sin-ta (Ottertail Valley).

On April 1, 1866, one chief, Wa-su-e-de-ya (Sets Fire to Hail) and nine men were assigned to this post. Wa-su-e-de-ya did not live long after he retired from scout service. Around May 1, 1869, he was scalped and killed by Chippewa Chief Flat Mouth and his band near Toqua (present-day Graceville, Minnesota).

Central Scout Camps

Big Island Scout Station

Big Island, the largest of several islands in Big Stone Lake, is approximately one hundred acres in size. Big Stone Lake, on the border of Minnesota and South Dakota, is about twenty-six miles long and about one to one and a half miles wide. Big Island, sometimes called Chamberlain Island, was named for an early day settler. Michael Alard, scout courier, carried dispatches and information between Fort Wadsworth and Fort Ridgely, Minnesota. This halfway station was operating as late as December 15, 1865.

Buzzard's Roost Scout Camp

Buzzard's Roost, the ninth camp set up in Dakota Territory, was also known as Hawk's Nest or Hechaote. It was established on top of a hill on May 15, 1865, in what is now Scotland Township, Day County. Solomon Two Stars was appointed chief of scouts.

The chiefs of each scout camp were given small mirrors to be used

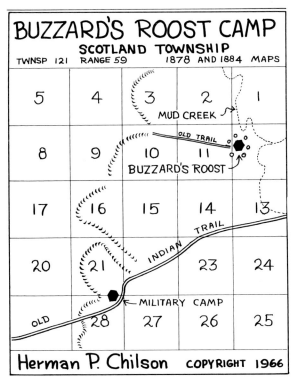

Buzzard's Roost Camp.

21

to signal for help. Two Stars and four of his scouts were patrolling the area on May 16, 1865, when five hostile Indians were spotted. Two Stars used a mirror to flash a signal for help. Inihan, chief of scouts at nearby Drifting Guts Camp, and four of his scouts rode over to help.

Two Stars and his scouts covered themselves with grass and lay down on the prairie. They were so concealed that the five Santee Sioux hostiles walked right into the trap. Four were killed immediately. However, the scouts had used up their ammunition, and the fifth hostile, Standing Cloud, stole a pony from one of the scouts and fled. This incident took place two miles northwest of present-day Webster, South Dakota.

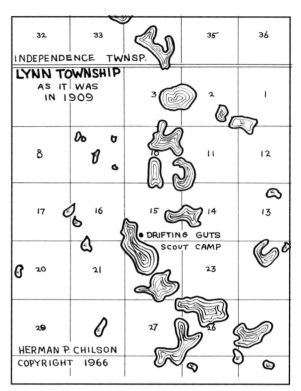

Drifting Guts Scout Camp.

These hostiles were members of the Campbell party that killed Andrew J. Jewett and his family in Garden City, Blue Earth County, Minnesota, on May 2, 1865. John L. (Jack) Campbell, leader of the party, had been caught and tried and was being held in jail when the townspeople lynched him. The other five members of the party fled into Dakota Territory with the stolen goods from the Jewett home.

During the fight, one of the hostiles ran up to Solomon Two Stars and begged for mercy. He recognized his sister's son. Solomon told him he loved him, but he remembered his oath and his orders, and he told his men to shoot him. (Another version of this story says he shot before the tears dimmed his eyes). Two Stars did not speak English but Victor Renville, son of Gabriel Renville, was his interpreter. Two of the scouts were wounded during this incident, but not seriously.

Sam Brown's version of this incident varies a little. According to him, the scouts had only one casualty, James Itewanyaka (Hewayaka). In his hurry to fire at a hostile, James overloaded his rifle; it exploded and blew off part of his hand. A week later Sam took him to Fort Wadsworth where Doctor Charles I. Farley amputated his hand. After that, he became known as 'One-Armed Jim'.

James could not be put to sleep with ether so Doctor Farley had to use chloroform. That was a recent discovery that had been used extensively during the Crimean War. This was possibly the first time chloroform was used in this area.

Drifting Guts Scout Camp

Drifting Guts Camp was established May 14, 1865, on Lynn Lake in present-day Day County. Inihan, a fullblood who served in General Sibley's 1863 Expedition, was the chief of scouts. This camp was known to the Indians as Xupeichoge, (Shupeechogee) , meaning 'drifting guts', so named because guts had been found drifting onto the shore.

Huge herds of buffalo were often found at the Lynn Lake area during the 1860s. On June 9, 1865, Sam Brown brought twenty-two men from Fort Wadsworth to hunt buffalo in this area.

Wabé Scout Camp

Wabé Scout Camp was created when the military scouting line was moved farther east. Major Brown suggested that the scouts serving at Fort Ridgely move to a line starting at Lake Benton, up the Sioux River to Lake Kampeska, then to Enemy Swim and on to Lake Traverse. Hawk's Nest, Drifting Guts, Head of the Coteau and Dry Wood Lake camps were all abandoned then.

On October 26, 1865, Major Brown appointed Solomon Two Stars as chief of scouts. Wabé Scout Camp was located at the site of where present-day Sandy Beach is on Enemy Swim Lake in Day County, South Dakota.

The spelling and pronunciation of Wabé has changed through the years by white settlers. First, it was Wabé, then Wahbay, and then Wau-bay with the accent on the first syl-

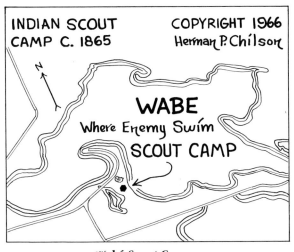

Wabé Scout Camp.

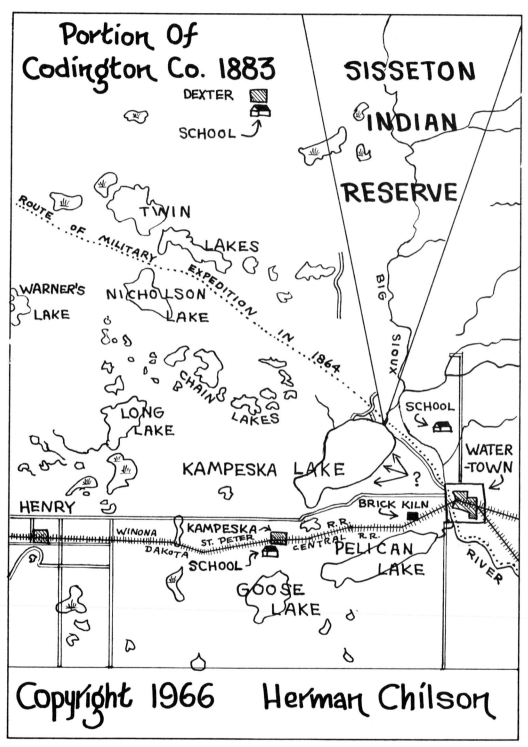

Portion Of Codington Co. 1883

DEXTER

SCHOOL →

SISSETON INDIAN RESERVE

ROUTE ... OF ... MILITARY ... EXPEDITION ... IN ... 1864

TWIN LAKES

WARNER'S LAKE

NICHOLSON LAKE

BIG Sioux

CHAIN LAKES

LONG LAKE

SCHOOL

KAMPESKA LAKE

?

WATER-TOWN

HENRY

BRICK KILN →

WINONA

KAMPESKA
ST. PETER

R.R.

DAKOTA
SCHOOL

CENTRAL R.R.

PELICAN LAKE

RIVER

GOOSE LAKE

Copyright 1966 Herman Chilson

Lake Kampeska Scout Camp.

24

lable. According to Riggs Dictionary, Wabé means a 'hatching place' and is pronounced Wa-baý.

Lake Kampeska Scout Camp

The Indians found an abundance of white shells on the lake shores and named this Lake Kampeska, meaning 'chinaware or white ware'. Years later, a scout camp was located at Lake Kampeska, north of present-day Watertown, South Dakota.

Very little is known about this camp. Henry Belland, Chief of Scouts at Fort Ridgely, Minnesota, in 1865, was in charge of the scouts stationed at Lake Kampeska and other locations in Dakota Territory and Minnesota.

Northern Scout Camps

Camp at White Bear Den, Dakota Territory. Photographers Illingsworth and Bill took this photo in 1866 while traveling with the Fisk Expedition.

The Montana Historical Society, Helena.

Bears Den Scout Camp

Major Joseph R. Brown established Bears Den in October 1865, with Ix-akiye as chief with thirteen scouts under him. Bears Den, sometimes known by its Indian name, Matoti, was located on a hill along the Sheyenne River in present-day Ransom County, North Dakota. This hill was well-known to the Indians since their sacred stone, Writing Rock, was located in the large ravine west of Fort Ransom.

One of Captain Fisk's emigrant wagon trains headed to the gold fields in Montana and stopped at Bears Den in June 1866. On June 30, Robert Fisk's diary entry stated:

> Broke camp at 6 1/2 o'clock. Marched 6 miles, lunched, and baited the cattle. Moved at one o'clock, and reached "Bears Den" (a range of high hills so designated on the map), at 5 o'clock, having made an afternoon's march 9 2/3 miles. Total distance traveled today 15 2/3 miles. The country over which we have passed to-day has been rolling prairie. Grass and water good and in abundance. At Bears Den an excellent spring of limestone water was found in a deep ravine beneath the brow of the neighboring hillside. *Robert Fisk Diary, James Liberty Fisk and Family Papers, Volume 2, Minnesota Historical Society*

Fort Wadsworth's Commander, Captain Crossman was ordered to take command of the Tenth Infantry on June 18, 1867, march to Bears Den and build a two- company post. General A. H. Terry and staff from Fort Snelling, Minnesota were on an inspection tour and met Captain Crossman of Bears Den. General Terry selected the spot where the post should be set up. During the summer, with the help of a few civilians, they built a bake house, hospital, quartermaster's warehouse, officer's and men's quarters and two blockhouses on which were mounted two howitzers.

Head of Coteau Scout Camp

Charles Crawford, chief of scouts, had ten scouts at Head of Coteau Scout Camp located on the northernmost point of the Coteau des Prairies on Sprague Lake, about three miles southwest of present-day Rutland, North Dakota. This camp was considered very necessary after Gabriel Renville moved his camp from Skunk Lake to the James River. There would have been too large an area exposed between the post on the Sheyenne River and Surrendered Camp.

While on an early morning patrol on May 18, 1865, Charles Crawford and five scouts came upon eight hostiles. Led by Black Legs, they were on their way to Minnesota on a horse stealing expedition. After an exciting running fight that lasted several hours and took the scouts twenty-five miles from their camp, three of the hostiles were killed.

A few months after this incident, the camp was broken up and moved to Bone Hill.

Maple River Scout Camp

Maple River Scout Camp was first mentioned February 15, 1866, when Major Brown suggested reorganizing the scout camps. He appointed one chief and fourteen men to the camp. Maple River Camp was located six miles northwest of present-day Leonard, North Dakota. Between 1867 and 1868, the name was changed to Maple River Station. The United States Government hired one half-breed scout, his wife and one soldier from Fort Totten to man the post.

In January 1870, James R. Wilson was the stationkeeper at Maple River and William Courselle was in charge of the station. In 1872, it was called Wilson Mail Station on the sectional map of Dakota Territory.

Sheyenne River Scout Camp

This camp was situated about ten miles southeast of present-day Lisbon, North Dakota, on the south side of the big bend of the Sheyenne River. On October 21, 1865, Major Brown appointed Tonkonxaiciye (Sacred Stone That Paints Itself Red) chief of scouts with six scouts to assist him. They served until December when they were discharged for the winter months. On February 15, 1866, this camp was staffed with one chief and fourteen scouts.

The Sibley Expedition of 1863 camped on the north side of the Sheyenne River across the river from the future campsite. Protestant missionary Steven Return Riggs,traveled with the Sibley Expedition and sent back reports to the newspapers describing this site as the most beautiful one they had seen on the trail.

Skunk Lake Scout Camp

The first officially designated scout camp in Dakota Territory was established at Skunk Lake in October 1863. Known today as Lake Tewaukon, the camp was located at the northernmost point of the Coteau des Prairies about six miles south of present-day Cayuga, North Dakota. Gabriel Renville was the first chief of scouts serving from October 14, 1863 to 1865. There were ninety three people at this camp: Renville, twenty one scouts, thirty six women and thirty five children. At that time the scouts received no pay, just rations for themselves and their families.

An artist's drawing of Captain Fields and his company in the disastrous blizzard near the Twin Lakes Scout Camp. Privates Maxwell and Crop took turns using whips to keep the men moving.

Moses-Kimball Armstrong Papers. Vol. 5, Clipping Scrapbook. 1872-1884, 1898.
Minnesota Historical Society.

A stone and bronze marker, erected in 1972 on the east side of the lake, designates the campsite of General Sibley's Expedition on July 2, 1863.

Twin Lakes Station

Fort Wadsworth's closest link to civilization was Fort Abercrombie seventy-six miles away. In the winter, that distance was too far to travel without a midway stopping point. In October 1864, Major Rose sent Chief of Scouts Pierre Bottineau and six scouts to put up a temporary shelter for the scouts, mail carriers and their horses at Lightning's Nest (the proper name was Thunder Nest). Bottineau informed Major Rose that he could find a shorter route, thus not crossing the Wild Rice River twice. Since the soldiers were still building their quarters and were weakened by leading escort and patrol detachments, Major Rose couldn't spare any men for building at the halfway site; the work was assigned to the troops from Fort Abercrombie.

In November 1864, the Commander of Fort Abercrombie, Lieutenant Colonel Powell Adams, sent a detachment of thirty-five men of Company B, Hatch's Battalion of the Minnesota Voluntary Cavalry, under Captain G. C. Whitcomb, to build and garrison the new station.

The men lived in tents while they cut timber and built stables and living quarters. However, they rejected the Lightning's Nest site, choosing instead an elevated area several miles away, close to Moran's Lake. Known as Twin Lakes Station, it was located about six miles southwest of present-day Hankinson, North Dakota.

Within the next three years, tragedy struck twice at this site. The first incident occurred around Christmas Day, 1864, when five soldiers, three double teams of horses and three sleds left Fort Abercrombie with supplies for Fort Wadsworth. The trail was marked with four foot stakes with black rags tied on top. It took two days to reach the Twin Lakes Station, where they spent the night. On the way to Fort Wadsworth they were caught in a blizzard. They dug into snowbanks and lived on crackers and frozen salt pork. One of the men dug holes in the lakes, scooped out water and made coffee, after boiling out the alkali. They survived, but all suffered from the bitter cold and exposure.

The second tragedy occurred February 1866. Captain Albert R. Field of Company A, Second Minnesota Cavalry, was ordered to take some soldiers and march from Fort Wadsworth to Sauk Centre, Minnesota. On February 12, 1866, Field sent a detachment of men under Lieutenant William Briley on ahead. He followed with twenty-eight men the next day. The weather was fine until they were thirteen miles from the Twin Lakes Station, and it started to snow. Captain Field

Andrew J. Fisk (known as Jack), age 14, served with the Sully Expedition of 1864. He then served three years with the Second Minnesota Cavalry on the Minnesota and Dakota frontier.

Montana Historical Society, Helena.

took three men and an extra horse and went on ahead to get the fire going and have food ready for the men. The snow turned into a raging blizzard so fierce that the horses refused to move. Lieutenant Stevens and his men turned back to the foot of the Coteau Hills and buried themselves in the snow. Corporal Lysander G. Harkness died that night in the blizzard. The rest returned to Fort Wadsworth. Captain Field and the three men with him (Charles Fertile, Curtis Smith, and Philo Walker) all perished in the storm. Search parties were sent out to find their bodies. Charles Fertile's body was found on March 6 about eight miles from the Twin Lakes Station. The search finally ended May 1 when the bodies of Captain Field and Curtis Smith were found fifteen miles southwest of Twin Lakes Station. Philo Walker's body was never found.

One of the men ordered to go with Captain Fields was Andrew J. Fisk. He recorded the tragic events in his diary.

> Tuesday, February 13, 1866. Foot of the Coteau—was up and had breakfast at two o'clock. Got saddled up (some of us bro't our horses in the quarters and saddled them) and started at 3 o'clock. Got to the foot of the Coteau at 9 & left at 11. Capt. Field—C. Smith—P. J. C. Walker—& C. L. Fertile left us to go ahead to Twin Lake from the Coteau. Met Col. Smith's party about a mile from the Coteau. We got out about 10 miles & were caught in a terrible snowstorm—lost the road—boys commenced freezing badly—had to turn back. Lt. and 12 of us managed to get into the foot of the Coteau—about dark— "Pap" French & Numner got in a little later—badly chilled. The rest of the boys on the prairie I expect, looks dubious. Bitter cold. 35° below zero. Clothes all froze stiff to us—nothing to eat. God help our poor boys on the prairie.

> Wednesday, February 14, Terrible long cold night. All we could do to keep from freezing to death. The rest of the boys were on the prairie all night about 2 miles from here. Ly Harkness froze to death and a good many badly frozen. We were all day getting them and our teams into the Coteau. Austin Maxwell acted like a hero last night on the prairie—used the mule whip and kept the boys from freezing to death. Dist. some coffee and frozen bread about noon. Have got the tents up and frozen boys as well taken care of as possible. Baidy—Wilson—Kline—Luijden—Polson & Ide frozen badly—besides some of the recruits belonging to Cos. 'H' and 'K' who are with us. Sat up until 12 1/2 o'clock drying my clothes. Some of the boys are badly discouraged 38° below.

> Thursday, February 15, Ft. Wadsworth D. T.
> Thank God we are once more by a warm fire. We put all the badly frozen

boys in one sleigh this morning—and Lt. & I started ahead to hurry out help for the boys.

We came in in 1$^{1}/_{4}$ hour—at 11 o'clock. And most of the mounted men soon after. Capt. Davy with several teams started out immediately & met the team about 6 miles out & brought them in all right. 5 men in hospital. We are in our old quarters. We left everything we had at the foot of the Coteau. Have not heard a word from Capt. Field & the boys yet—are afraid they are frozen to death. Mrs. Capt. Davy gave me a good dinner—came near fainting away when I got by a warm fire. *Andrew Jackson Fisk Diary, 1864-1866, from the Fisk Family Papers, Manuscript Collection 31, Montana Historical Society Archives, Helena, Montana.*

After March 10, 1866, soldiers were not stationed there; the post was manned by half-breed scouts. Xavier Moran (for whom the lake was named) was still stationed at Twin Lakes in 1880, hauling supplies from Breckenridge, Minnesota to Fort Sisseton (the name was changed in 1876). Moran's job was eliminated in 1881 when the Chicago, Milwaukee, St. Paul Railroad reached Webster, South Dakota. Supplies were then hauled from Webster to Fort Sisseton.

James River Scout Camps

Elm River Scout Camp

The first site of the Elm River Scout Camp was at the mouth of the Elm River in February 1865. Inihan was appointed chief of scouts in October that year. Major Brown planned to have more than one campsite on the Elm River, but Military Headquarters did not approve his plan, so he had to settle on just one site.

Major Brown moved the camp to a site nine miles southwest of present-day Frederick, South Dakota, on February 17, 1866. This was considered the head of the Elm River. Joseph Rouillard was appointed chief of scouts on April 16, 1866, with nine scouts under him. This was the former site of Colin Campbell's fur trading post and the former location of Chief Waneta and his band of Yanktonai Sioux.

Herman Chilson's research of reports, letters, and maps of Joseph R. Brown, Samuel J. Brown, Charles E. Jewett, John Hunter and William O'Toole appear to establish the location of the Elm River Scout Camp at the head of the

Elm River in the spring and summer of 1866. It was here, at the second site of Elm River Scout Camp, that Samuel Brown rode when he made that ride on April 19, 1866, to deliver a message that hostiles were approaching. Because the message was false, Brown immediately exchanged his pony for another and returned to Fort Wadsworth. He was caught in a spring blizzard on the way back. His story is at the end of this chapter.

Lieutenant Charles E. Jewett of Company C, Tenth Infantry, arrived at Rouillard's camp on June 10, 1866. Here they established a camp that provided protection for the emigrants and settlers and remained for the summer.

Bone Hill Scout Camp

Bone Hill Camp (Huhupaha) was set up on the west side of the James River two or three miles south of present-day LaMoure, North Dakota. Charles Crawford, former chief of scouts at the Head of the Coteau Camp, was appointed chief of scouts at Bone Hill on October 31, 1865.

Bone Hill derived its name from the hundreds of buffalo bones found on top of this hill. Sam Brown reported seeing a three-foot ring of small bones from the front legs and the back of the shins of the buffaloes on this hill.

Several large expeditions stopped at Bone Hill on their journey westward. On July 3, 1866, another one of Captain Fisk's wagon trains stopped here on the way to the gold fields in Montana. It took them an hour and a half to cross the James River because they had to stop to fix the crossing. According to Fisk, the James River was forty yards wide and two feet deep. The next day, July 4, they celebrated by killing twenty-five buffaloes.

Bone Hill Scout Camp closed April 5, 1866, making Elm River Scout Camp the farthest west of all the scout camps.

James River Scout Camp

After Major Brown was appointed Special Military Agent in charge of the scouting program, he ordered Gabriel Renville to close the Skunk Lake Camp and set up a new camp on the James River on September 14, 1864. It was located on the east side of the James River near a cottonwood grove. This was also known as Cottonwood Grove, Cottonwood Point and Renville's Camp. Gabriel Renville was chief of scouts here with thirty-nine scouts working under him, making this the largest of all scout camps. On October 17, 1864, the force was reduced to twelve scouts and then increased to thirty-five by December that year.

This camp was located six miles west and five miles north of present-day Groton, South Dakota. It was chosen for the large grove of trees and huge herds of buffalo.

Oak Grove Scout Camp

Another camp located on the James River was Oak Grove, known by the Indians as Utohozhu. Oak Grove was located seven miles east and five miles south of present-day Warner, South Dakota. E-chana-ji-ka was chief of scouts.

During 1865, between 150 and 200 lodges of Yanktonai Sioux and their chief Mdoka camped at the site. Several lodges of Uncpapa and several bands of Teton Sioux also camped here.

On March 1, 1865, Samuel J. Brown was ordered by Major Robert H. Rose to proceed to Oak Grove to arrest a Red River half-breed who was reported to be trading with some Indians and giving them whiskey. He was accompanied by six scouts and six soldiers under the command of Lieutenant Thomas Thompson.

They traveled all night, going past the scout camps at Cottonwood Grove, down the James River by Moccasin Creek, and arriving at Oak Grove Scout Camp early the next morning. About 150 lodges of Yanktonnai's Sioux were camped there buffalo hunting.

The man they were sent to arrest, Antoine Beaulieu from Fort Abercrombie, was there trading gun powder, brass buttons, and other trinkets for buffalo skins and robes. After each purchase, he would give each customer a small bottle of what he called "woya zan kte"(pain killer), which was really bad whiskey which he used as Sinte. (In Sioux, Sinte means 'tail end'. It was the custom for Indian traders to give something to induce the customers to come again.)

The arrest was made.

Moccasin River Scout Camp

The camp, spelled "Mockinson" in the official records, was set up about seven miles north of Oak Grove Scout Camp at the mouth of Moccasin Creek. The first listing on December 2, 1865, showed eight scouts serving both Elm River and Moccasin River Scout Camps. Then on February 15, 1866, Major Brown appointed one chief and fourteen scouts to man the post.

Snake Creek Scout Camp

Sam Brown
Chilson Photo Collection

Major Brown established Snake Creek Scout Camp in May 1865. Snake Creek was known as Wamsdukuyu by the Indians, meaning "Made Blind by the Bite of a Snake". It was located opposite Snake Creek, six miles north of present-day Redfield, South Dakota, on the north or east side of the James River. E-chana-ji-ka (Stands Easy), a soldier of the Rattling Mockinson's Band of the Sisseton Sioux was appointed chief of scouts here with seven men under him.

Another camp listed in 1866 was Turtle Creek Scout Camp located three miles northeast of present-day Redfield, South Dakota. It was located on John and Christian Hagman's farm in a large grove of trees where Turtle Creek empties into the James River. Sometimes known as Camp Hagman, it was possibly a subcamp under the chief of scouts at Snake Creek Camp. No record was found of a chief for Turtle Creek Scout Camp.

The Fort Ridgely cluster of scout camps included Thompson, Tetonkaha, Hendricks, Shakotan, Lake Benton, Medary, Artichoke, Hawk Creek, Rice Creek and Renshaw, which were located south and east of Fort Wadsworth, with some also in Minnesota. These camps were similar to the ones further north. The families accompanied the scouts and received food, clothing and rations, besides horses and ammunition when necessary. The difference was that the southern scouts had a more leisurely lifestyle. The northern scouts were required to work all day, while the southern scouts did a limited amount of scouting, leaving time for hunting and fishing, which the northern scouts were not allowed to do so while on duty. The northern scouts were paid monthly wages, whereas these scouts drew only rations, but no pay. Only their chief was paid.

Major Brown was instrumental in selecting the sites and appointing scouts at these scout camps in the Fort Ridgely cluster.

There were times when problems arose with the scouts. In August 1864, Major Clowney, Commandant at Fort Wadsworth, discharged one of the scouts, Mark Wells, for general bad conduct, neglect of duty, abuse of his horse, making false reports and being totally unreliable. Major Rose was sometimes upset with the scouts because the mail was so slow in arriving. In 1875 two Indian scouts, Caska and Oieyica, ran off with one horse. A reward of $30.00 was posted.

Another incident occurred in May 1873, when ten scouts and their leader, Louis Dumarce, threatened to leave and then did so. Each man had a carbine, a revolver and ammunition. Three scouts returned to the fort and surrendered themselves to the commandant. When the others failed to return, several soldiers were ordered to capture them and bring them back. The scouts were found eight or ten miles from the fort and were returned and placed in irons. After a discussion, the commander, Major J. E. Yard, ordered them released.

For the most part, however, the scouts were highly praised and much appreciated. Major Rose's admiration of the scouts is evident in the following excerpt from a letter written to Assistant General R. C. Olin on May 1, 1865:

...I would rather have one hundred of these scouts than a full regiment of cavalry. I would repeat previous suggestions that the chief of each set be increased to $2.00 per day and that Renville be raised to $3.00 per day. He is a very valuable man. I have increased the scouts force to 75, disposed of them as follows: Gabriel Renville, Chief of Scouts; Samuel J. Brown, Interpreter and chief of scouts, stationed at this post and the mail service. There are twelve in a mail service, they make two trips a week to Abercrombie, four to go with the mail to the halfway station. So making six in each set of couriers. While carrying the mail, they do the double duty of patrolling the country between here and Abercrombie. Twelve are stationed at this post, four remain in camp for any emergency and eight scout the country here thoroughly every day at the head of the Coteau. A chief and fifteen men, five to remain and guard the camp and the sets of five scout every day; at the Hawks Nest a chief and 18 men, six to remain in camp and two sets of six each scout every day and patrol the country to the junction of the James and Snake Rivers where I understand is the west boundary of this sub-district. A chief (Red Feather) and four in charge of encampment, five at the Agency, but to be constantly on the move visiting the different posts etc.

The scout's loyalty and devotion to duty was evident in numerous incidents. The story of Sam Brown's ride is an excellent example. Sam had served as a scout, interpreter, and inspector of scouts at Fort Wadsworth. On April 13, 1866, only six days before the ride, Sam was ordered to be the Chief of Scouts.

The following story is in Sam's words from the United States Senate Document No. 23. The story relates the events of that ride that left Sam unable to walk without crutches the rest of his life:

On the afternoon of April 19, 1866, at the military agency, near Fort Wadsworth, Dak. T., I received information that led me to believe there was imminent danger of an Indian raid. News was brought in to the effect that fresh moccasin tracks had been discovered in the vicinity of "where they cut bows" (now Jamestown, N. D.) on the upper James River, a few days before, and that the tracks led in the direction of the Minnesota frontier.

I immediately reported the matter to the commanding officer at the fort and informed him that I should at once leave for the Elm River for the purpose of putting the Scouts there on the qui vive. I was under most stringent orders not only from the lieutenant-colonel commanding at Fort Abercrombie, who required me to "see that all war parties are promptly pursued and intercepted in their hostile designs against the exposed frontiers of Minnesota and Iowa" (Circular Orders, No. 3, of April 5, 1866,) but also from the major-general commanding at St. Paul, who required me to "keep the scouts constantly on the qui vive." I therefore hurriedly drew on my buffalo skin suit—jacket, leggings, and moccasins—buckled a Henry to my waist belt, hurriedly bridled and saddled my horse, which stood in the stable near by and always kept ready for emergency of this kind that might arise and mounting the animal and giving it the whip, started off on a brisk gallop for the Elm River scouting station—between 55 and 60 miles away to the westward.

This scouting station was occupied by 17 lodges of scouts—regular and supernumerary—the former getting a per diem and rations and the latter rations only, and was under Joseph Rouillard, chief of scouts. The camp was located on the Elm River, about where Ordway, Brown County, S. Dak., now is, and was regarded as one of the most important outposts in the service. [This is an error; the site is 9 miles southwest of present-day Frederick, South Dakota near the southwest corner, Section 30, Township 127, Range 64.] Its location was far out in the hostile country and on the thoroughfare of travel for war parties from the northwest.

I left the fort, or rather the military agency half a mile east of it, at about sundown, and before I had gone far was enveloped in darkness. Indeed, when I reached the western edge of the Coteau Hills, 8 miles, utter darkness was upon me. The country from here on was a wild, level plain and almost trackless. I tried to follow an old trail which led to the Cottonwood Grove on the James and could not. But I had been over the route before and had no trouble in making my way, and, owing to the darkness, I felt safe from ambush.

The north star, which peered through the clouds at intervals, was my main reliance. It was my only guide and comforter. I galloped on at a rapid pace across this wild and trackless prairie country without any interval of rest or let up whatever, except when fording the James or pulling up the horse for a moment at a time to

Sam Brown's Ride, April 1866. Robert Widmeier, Artist.

South Dakota Game, Fish & Parks.

enable it to catch its breath, and arrived at my destination about midnight, making the distance, about 55 miles, in about five hours.

Entering the camp and going direct to the chief's lodge I dismounted and proceeded to tie the horse to a wagon near by when Rouillard, who had been lying under it, watching my movements, rose up and called out, "Hello Sam! What's up?" I hurriedly explained matters and was quickly informed that the Indians who had been sent north a month or so before as peace messengers to the hostile Sioux had that evening passed by on their return to the Cottonwood Grove on the James, and that they had assured him peace had been made and there was no longer any danger from Indian raids.

My father having been appointed a special agent of the Interior Department to collect the Minnesota Sioux and assemble them at Fort Rice to meet the United States peace commissioners there, had dispatched some trusty Indian messengers to the north to endeavor to negotiate and bring them in. These were the peace messengers referred to.

I was struck dumb with surprise and mortification, for I was satisfied I had come on a wild-goose chase, and the alarm was a false one; that no war party was coming, and that the tracks or the trail of these Indian messengers had been seen and supposed to be the tracks of hostile Indians. I at once decided to return without delay. I deemed it my duty to return at once and intercept the communication which I had sent in previous to my departure relative to hostile Indians, or to correct the same so as to not create unnecessary alarm at headquarters in St. Paul and throughout western Minnesota, the raid the spring before, particularly at the time of the murder of the Jewett family, near Mankato, and the capture and hanging of the half-breed Jack Campbell there having thrown the whole country into a feverish state of excitement and nervousness.

Besides, it was considered hazardous and foolhardy in the extreme to attempt to cross the prairies by day especially when alone, owing to the danger of being ambushed and waylaid by prowling Indians. So after securing Rouillard's fresh Indian pony, which stood picketed near the lodge, and which the chief had recommended as "tough and gamy" and saddling and bridling it, and giving my own horse a parting tap with the whip, I mounted the pony and dashed away in the night, homeward bound.

There was no moon or star to be seen, and I was enveloped in utter darkness. The north star, which had peered through the clouds and had guided and comforted me on the way over, was now completely hidden behind heavy clouds, and I was left with absolutely nothing to steer by except occasional faint flashes of lightning behind me in the west; and although the dark and heavy clouds overhead, as well as in the west, indicated a storm, I was not in the least disturbed thereby, and pushed forward in the direction of the James. When I had been out an hour or so, however, and had reached the river, and had heard the noise of the rushing waters before me, and the rumbling of thunder overhead and behind me, accompanied by sharp flashes of lightning, and felt a few drops of rain, I became somewhat nervous.

But when I had forded the stream and had struck an old and well-beaten trail and had recognized the spot where I, with a few scouts and a supply train, and Lieut. Jonathan Darrow with part of a company of soldiers, had camped a few nights before, and had found myself fairly on the James River flat, where the country before me was as level as a barn floor and free from wolf holes or gopher knolls or other impediments to fast traveling, I was not only delighted, but highly elated and very much encouraged, for I felt that I could keep ahead of any storm that might come up from the west. I whipped up the pony and dashed forward at a breakneck speed, and kept on at a very rapid pace until I had reached "the old hay meadow," a lake about halfway between the James River and the fort.

Here I heard "the voice of the Great Spirit issuing from the dark clouds of the west" in a more astounding tone than before. The flashes of lightning were so blinding and the peals of thunder so deafening that I made up my mind I would stop and crawl in among the tall reeds or rushes which skirted the lake and wait there for the rain to pass by, and pulled up.

I was about to alight when the thought all of a sudden struck me that some war party passing along might already have taken refuge there, and acting upon the maxim that "discretion is the better part of valor" I struck the pony with my rawhide whip and went flying past the reeds and on over the prairie at a rate that would have put a Giplin, a Sheridan, or a Rankin to the blush. I had proceeded but half a mile or so when there rushed upon me from behind one of the most terrific windstorms I ever knew. It rushed upon me with such suddenness and terrific force and violence that I was startled and nearly unhorsed.

Very soon the rain came. And such rain! It fairly poured. The floodgates of heaven seemed to have broken loose.

Following the rain and close upon it came sleet, hail, and snow, which in a few minutes turned into a snowstorm—a genuine Dakota blizzard.

Death stared me in the face and my situation was most awful. The terrible roar of the wind, the inky blackness of the night, and the thought of becoming lost or frozen or waylaid and scalped, and be given a sepulcher such as the wolves give, all combined, was terrible in the extreme. I need a "pencil and a pen divine" to describe it and do it justice. There was nothing to be seen, nothing to be felt or heard, save wind and snow. But in spite of this I managed to keep the wind to my back and pushed on, or, more properly speaking, the wind kept to my back and pushed me on, nolens volens.

Of course, no landmarks could be seen, but I knew, or thought I knew, that the range of hills known as the Coteau des Prairie was before me across my way, and that I needed only to be guided by the wind to reach it. I felt that once among the hills I could find shelter in one of the numerous wooded ravines or coulees there and be safe.

Very soon my clothes began to freeze, and notwithstanding my thick clothing, which kept my skin dry, I was decidedly uncomfortable.

My pony was truly "tough and gamy," as Rouillard had said it was, and it galloped on and on in the midst of the driving rain, sleet, hail, snow, and through slush and mud, and across swollen streams, and frozen and icy places. The noble little animal would sometimes gallop through the rushing water, sometimes slip and slide on frozen and icy places, and sometimes break through soft ice and dump me into the water. Twice I was thus thrown, but fortunately my hair lariat, one end of which was fastened to the bridle bit and the other tucked in under my belt, prevented the pony from getting away.

At about daybreak I found myself at the foot of the Coteau Hills—the western slope—which I ascended. On reaching the top I found that the storms had not only not abated, but seemed to have increased in fury—that is, the winds blew more furiously and the cold was more intense, but the snow was lighter and the air much clearer.

Landmarks could be seen. I discovered several familiar and noteworthy ones. Away to the northwest and about a mile distant is the ravine or coulee where Lieut. Thomas Thompson, of the Second Minnesota Cavalry, with a detachment of 15 or

"I found that I was about 25 miles southwest of the fort...."

20 soldiers and a dozen scouts and myself, camped of a night the spring before, after wandering about on the prairie all day in search of Indians. There, just to the southeast and about 5 miles away, is the butte or high peak overlooking the James River flats, and called (in official dispatches) Hawk's Nest or Buzzard's Roost. And there down on the flats, and about 3 miles away, is the spot where General Corse and staff and party of hunters from St. Paul, and a number of the officers and some of the scouts and soldiers and Indian hunters from Fort Wadsworth, the fall before, struck an immense herd of buffalo, estimated at 30,000 strong where a sprig of an officer on the general's staff who had evidently never seen a buffalo before got excited and accidentally shot his horse in the back of the head with his revolver and felled it to the ground and lost the day's sport—a never-ending joke on the fellow; and where on the same hunt and chase a strange adventure befell me—was chased 3 miles and into camp by a wounded and maddened buffalo.

I found that I was about 25 miles southwest of the fort—15 miles or more off course. The wind having shifted from the west to the northwest or north, I had without knowing it changed my own course correspondingly. So fierce was the wind that I dreaded to face it—dreaded the long ride before me. The thought that possibly hostile Indians may be lurking in one of the wooded ravines nearby destroyed ideas of seeking refuge there, and whipping up the pony I dashed forward. The little fellow at first lagged and needed considerable urging. It, too, dreaded to

Brown went to Vasseur's lodge.

face the piercing wind. But it finally pricked up its ears and took the "dog trot" and kept it.

I was now shivering with cold and had well-nigh lost all hope. Giving the pony the reins and allowing it to jog along at its own gait and picking its own way, I sat shivering and wished I was at home. The noble little pony jogged along up hill and down, across frozen creeks, lakes, marshes, and swamps, until the fort, or rather the military agency, which I had left the evening before, was reached, about 8 o'clock on the morning of April 20, 1866, having traveled about 150 miles during the night.

I proceeded directly to the agency building, or, more properly speaking, being "played out" the pony took me straight to it, and rode up to the stockade, which was built of substantial oak posts or pickets 10 feet high, around the building, with portholes for musketry and bastions or blockhouses at the angles, for the purpose of defense in case of attack from the Indians and dismounted, or rather rolled off the pony and fell in a heap on the ground, bereft of the use of my legs.

The muscles were perfectly relaxed, but I had no control over them. Gathering myself up by aid of the pony's forelegs and mane, I unbuckled the girth, took off the saddle and bridle, and let the animal go. I was completely wet through and shivering with cold, was weak, and in an exhausted condition, and as the pony struck out for the stable and haystack nearby I staggered toward the stockade gate and fell headlong through it and against the door of the house and burst it open. I crawled in and up to a bedtick in a corner of the room, where for hours, or until late in the afternoon of that day, I lay in a condition of semi-consciousness and stupor, which I arose Rip Van Winkle-like and left the house, and walked slowly and with difficulty and in a staggering manner to the tepee or lodge of Francois Vasseur, an old French trapper, frontiersman, and scout, about a quarter of a mile distant toward the fort, and there, suffering with aches and pains, and from a weak, exhausted feeling, and with all energy and courage lost, I sent for the commanding officer, Lieut. James E. Cochrane, of the Independent Battalion, Minnesota Cavalry, who immediately came to see me. I told him all about my trip and asked to be relieved from further duty for the reason that I was no longer fit for service. He promised to send at once (by courier) to Fort Abercrombie and correct the report I had made the day before relative to hostile Indians, and which had been forwarded that morning.

Prior to the ride and the hardships encountered, as herein set forth, I enjoyed good, sound physical health: was robust and strong, active, and energetic. When a schoolboy I could lift more, run faster, jump higher and farther than any of my schoolmates. At least, I thought I could. The boys of Old Seabury, at Faribault, and of Dixon College, at Paul, can testify as to that. Today I am a physical wreck, not having taken a natural step since the incurrence of my disabilities. I am compensated in a measure, however, by the reflection that I did my duty."

Known as the Paul Revere of the Prairie, Sam's heroic 150 mile ride accomplished little since the report of an impending raid was false. Because of his exposure to the cold, rain and sleet he said, "I contracted injuries which deranged my eyes, dimmed my eyesight, paralyzed my muscular powers, deprived me of the use of my legs, and all natural power of motion, and permanently impaired my general health."

The following affidavit was found in Sam Brown's personal papers:
Samuel J. Brown of Browns Valley, Minnesota.
  Brief of Affidavit of Dr. M. R. Wilcox of Henderson, Minn.
oOoOoOo

  Took charge of claimant and commenced treating him for paralysis about August 1st, 1866 and continued treating him up to about June 1st, 1867. There was paralysis of the lower extremities so that he could not use them at all. This was his condition when I first saw him in 1866. Disease increased effecting the whole system. After I took charge of and began treating him he was unable to feed himself or to use his hands and arms in any manner. I visited him twice a day at first for five

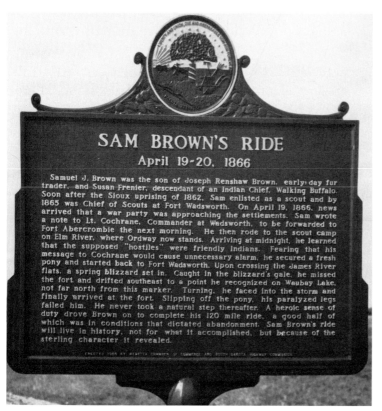

This historical marker on US Highway 12 informs travelers of Sam Brown's ride.

Chilson Photo Collection.

Sam Brown, the Prairie Paul Revere, was crippled as a result of his ride in 1866 to alert scouts and others of an impending raid that proved to be a false alarm.

Minnesota Historical Society.

43

months. At close of my treatment there had been some improvement, so much that claimant could walk a little by aid of crutches.

Have known claimant from his boyhood up–have been family physician of his father– the late Hon. Joseph R. Brown and I know claimant was a strong healthy young man before entering U. S. Service. Am satisfied that paralysis of claimant was caused by fatigue and exposure in U. S. Service. Saw him about two years ago. He could then walk with difficulty with two canes. He will never recover from this physical disability so as to enable him to perform any manual labor.

[Signed] M. R. Wilcox
Sworn to before Orrin Kipp, N. P.
Sibley County, Minn., Nov., 30, 1877.

Sam spent the remainder of his life living in Browns Valley, Minnesota. (When he moved there it was called Lac Travers, was later known as Lake Traverse, and in 1872 was named Browns Valley in memory of his father, Major Brown). Sam served as postmaster from 1867 to 1878. In 1869 he became the first notary public in the county. In 1872 Sam, Angus and Joseph Brown opened the first Real Estate office in Browns Valley, and later they operated a freighting business.

Sam married Phoebe Robinson in 1887. He died August 19, 1925.

Lieutenant John S. Allanson.
Chilson Photo Collection.

Lieutenant John S. Allanson became Acting Quartermaster in 1869. He assumed command of the scouts and the mounted force of the post. In November he took a detachment of soldiers to the Fort Ransom Road, placing sixty-six posts supported by four-foot mounds on all the prominent positions on the road one half mile apart. They also repaired old mounds and had a log bridge constructed up the stream at the head of the Coteau.

The three forts, Abercrombie, Ransom and Wadsworth, joined by straight lines, formed a triangle. The roads connecting these frontier posts were well marked by 1869 so they could be traveled in winter. Time of travel between any two of the posts was about two days.

On October 16, 1879, three officers, six enlisted men and Indian scout Sergeant James King (Akicitana) captured two escaped armed robbers and turned them over to civil authorities. These two robbers had attacked a Norwegian farmer in Minnesota and stolen his horses. The robbers then raced into nearby Ortonville where they rode up and down main street firing their weapons. They went into the saloon for more drinks, and one of the men shot himself in the foot while showing off his marksmanship skill. After the farmer was brought into town, the townspeople demanded the two bandits be captured. A posse was formed, and they were captured this first time in an empty claim shack out of town. They were arrested and fined by the local justice of the peace and released.

Grace Hall writes the following in her book, The Wadsworth Trail:

"He [the local justice of the peace] was probably too much in fear of them to punish them as they deserved. [In that town even] The bondsmen owned a disreputable saloon which bore the sign, 'Y.M.C.A.' in very large letters. In small letters, underneath, was printed 'Young man come again.' A crude welcome—but typical in those rough days."

"St. Paul papers published an account of this incident and so it came to the attention of United States Marshal Lewellyn of Iowa. He believed these bandits were men he was looking for, since men of their description had fled through Kansas, Nebraska, Iowa and southern Minnesota committing crimes of burglary, horse stealing, theft; the murder of a postmaster in Kansas and other homicides in Nebraska and Iowa. The marshal telegraphed the postmaster in Ortonville to arrest the men. Before the arrest was made the bandits learned of the message and left the village on horseback, stopping ten or twelve miles from Ortonville at a vacant cabin. A posse of fifteen or twenty men followed them, but after a severe bombardment at the cabin the outlaws made their escape into the Coteau des Prairies. The posse had to give up the chase and it was not until about two weeks later that the desperadoes were finally captured by a troop of soldiers from Fort Wadsworth. When taken into custody, each man had about $8,000 in currency on his person. They were taken back to the scenes of former crimes, convicted and hanged."

As time went on, there appeared to be less need for scouts, so on August 16, 1881, the Indian scouts were released from military service. Captain Bennet wrote, "Scout Akicitana was a great loss to the party: the loss of the use of his four horses to hunt for poles and settle questions of 'claims' was another loss. He is one of the best scouts I ever saw."

During the winter of 1882 Captain Bennet received permission to re-enlist Sergeant Akicitana (James King). He did not wish to bring his wife and children to the fort but instead wanted them to stay on his farm near Clear Lake and requested passes to go there. Akicitana had taken the name James King from Jay King, a young man who stayed at the fort and became his close friend.

Sergeant Akicitana had been a scout at the fort since 1871. He was a member of the Company B, Twenty-fifth Infantry, until his discharge on December 8, 1889. He served the longest time of any of the scouts and was the best known. Although he had a farm on Clear Lake, he was a missionary on the Pine Ridge Reservation in southern South Dakota from 1892 to 1920. He died on November 7, 1946, at the age of 101. Indian scouts continued to work at Fort Sisseton until 1889. In later years the scouts were used to catch deserters and arrest civilians cutting wood on the military reservations without permission.

Sergeant James King (Akicitana) served as a scout in Company B, Fort Sisseton Division, until his discharge in 1889. He died November 7, 1946, at age 101.

Johnson Photo Collection

Scout Camp Churches

Missionaries brought Christianity to the Indian people in Minnesota, Nebraska and Dakota Territory; as the Indians moved westward, so did the missionaries. The Reverend John P. Williamson, a Presbyterian missionary, was probably the first circuit rider in eastern Dakota Territory. He was the son of the Reverend Thomas P. Williamson, who organized the first church in Minnesota at Fort Snelling. The 1864 records reveal that the Reverend John Williamson stopped at the Skunk Lake Scout Camp in January and held a camp meeting on Sunday evening. The next morning he baptized the infant child of Solomon Two Stars and several other people. Solomon had been converted to Christianity several years before by Williamson and the Reverend Steven Return Riggs.

While at Skunk Lake Camp Williamson also visited the lodge of Simon Anawangmani (One Who Goes Galloping Upon). Simon, who had been converted to Christianity in 1840, was a licensed pastor. In the summer of 1866 Simon and Pierre Big Fire were licensed to preach in the scout camp near Fort Wadsworth.

The first ordained Indian minister was John Renville. Licensed to preach on May 1, 1865, and ordained that fall, the Reverend Renville preached to the scout camps from 1866 to 1868.

The Reverend Steven Return Riggs came to the nearby Sisseton-Wahpeton Indian Reservation in 1867. Along with Renville they held a large central meeting to administer the Lord's Supper. The four day camp meeting attracted Indians from a twenty-five mile area. In 1870 Riggs established the Goodwill Mission on the Sisseton-Wahpeton Indian Reservation and supervised the scout camp churches until he died in 1883. The six churches were Ascension, Goodwill, Long Hollow, Kettle Lake (near Fort Wadsworth), Buffalo Lake and White Banks. The total membership was about 350 people.

Reverend Stephen R. Riggs, a Presbyterian missionary, accompanied the Sisseton-Wahpeton delegation in 1867 to Washington, D.C., to make a treaty with the United States government. This resulted in the formation of the Sisseton-Wahpeton Reservation.

Minnesota Historical Society.

The army headquarters approved the work the Reverend Renville was doing and ordered Major Rose at Fort Wadsworth to see to it that Renville had all the proper facilities for preaching among the Indians at the fort.

The Scouts (Tonweya) Church was composed of Christian Indian scouts who patrolled the area from Fort Abercrombie to the Kettle Lakes area. The church existed from 1863 to 1868. Elders were Simon Anawangmani, Paul Mazakutemani, Antoine Renville and Napeshni. They had an average of thirty nine members.

The Kettle Lake (Cegaiyeyapi) Church was organized near Fort Wadsworth in August 1868. The church was composed of Fort Wadsworth scouts and their families. There were twenty-two members, some of them women.

Elders were David Grey Cloud and James Akicitana. The church members asked that Louis Mazawakinyanna (Little Iron Thunder) be ordained as their pastor. Mazawakinyanna was born in Shakopee's village in Minnesota. He took part in the Minnesota Uprising in 1862 and was sentenced to hang, but he was converted to Christianity and later pardoned by President Andrew Johnson. He became the first ordained minister at the Goodwill Mission on the Sisseton-Wahpeton Indian Reservation and also served as supply pastor at Kettle Lake, Buffalo Lake and other churches. In 1871, Mazawakinyanna was transferred to the Mayason Church, and David Tomhpeyahote was appointed pastor. On September 9, 1873, David Grey Cloud was ordained a minister. He had been preaching at the Kettle Lake Church since June 1873, drawing a salary of $104 a year. In 1877, Kettle Lake Church was consolidated with Buffalo Lake Church.

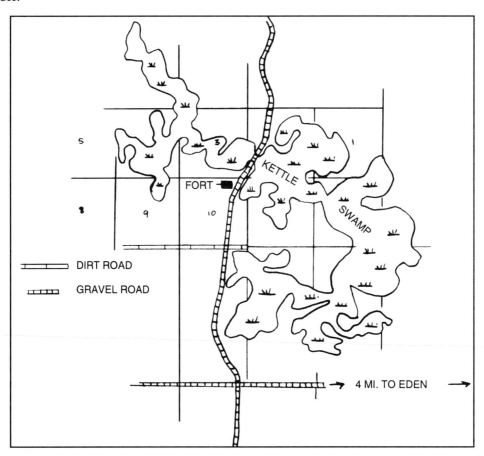

Fort Sisseton is located in Section 10, T-125-N, R-56-W, Fort Township, Marshall County, South Dakota. The roads have been upgraded since Herman Chilson drew this map.

Chilson Collection.

Chapter Three

Establishing Fort Wadsworth

"I am more and more satisfied that Fort Wadsworth will prove
to be one of the most important military stations in the northwest."
Brigadier General H. H. Sibley
November 17, 1864

As soon as the site for the new fort was official on August 1, 1864, the soldiers started hauling logs, sawing, burning lime, hauling rock and digging cellars. For protection they dug in a cannon at each of the four corners. The men, working under the direction of Assistant Quartermaster Captain J. E. McKusick, realized the necessity of constructing shelters before winter arrived. By the seventeenth of August, the men had the twenty-horsepower portable sawmill running. This machine proved to be a source of considerable encouragement to them.

In the meantime, Major Clowney checked out the timber in the coulees and the hay land in the surrounding area. He felt there was enough timber to build and maintain a fort. Although there was plenty of grass available, it was matted down with dead grass. The prairie grasses had not been burned off for some time, making it impossible for a mowing machine to be used. Suitable hay could be found at a further distance, but Major Clowney could not spare any of his men for the job of mowing. He accepted a deal offered by Mark Donnie to secure the hay if Major Clowney would furnish the machinery and guards. Thirty infantry, ten cavalry, one mountain howitzer, six men and four scouts under the command of Captain John Klatt left on the sixth of August with Donnie and the half-breeds he hired to cut hay, seventeen miles from the post.

While Major John Clowney and Captain J. E. McKusick were examining the land, trees and water in the area, they noted that the Kettle Lakes were horseshoe-shaped. They found two places where the lakes could be forded and one place, ten rods wide, for the loaded wagons to approach the fort site. However, they also discovered something they felt should be kept a secret.

In a private letter to General Sibley, dated August 10, 1864, Major Clowney stated he was sure there was coal in existence in the vicinity of Fort Wadsworth. Sibley's answer was

...You are right in keeping the matter from obtaining publicity, as the advantage, if any is to gained, should accrue to the Government in the first place, and the fact be communicated through the regular military channels, that the superior authorities in Washington may give the necessary directions. You will please therefore to advise me confidentially, after you have made the proposed explorations, of the result, and if the discovery proves to be valuable the report will be at once transmitted to department headquarters to be forwarded. In addition to your ordinary official dispatches, I shall be glad to receive an occasional private letter from you, giving such suggestions and information of matters about the post, etc., as might not be suited to an official letter. I shall be glad to receive such any time.

[Signed] H. H. Sibley, Brig. Gen.

No further mention was found regarding this find.

By September 1, Major John Clowney reported that the one-story blockhouses were completed. Timber was cut for the magazine so their ammunition could be stored. The blacksmith shop was completed, and a small building for the fort headquarters was nearly complete. Plans were underway to have the quartermaster's and commissary buildings ready in a short time. Any delays were attributed to the difficulties they encountered keeping the saw mill operational.

Erecting a log stockade around the post buildings was in the original plans; however, due to the lack of timber, plans were changed. Major Rose ordered the men to dig a ditch ten feet wide around the post. The earth was then piled up on the inside, forming an embankment about eight feet high. On top of this were placed two eight-inch wooden beams with holes in the bottom beams for muskets.

While the infantry was busy constructing buildings, the scouts and cavalry were on guard duty, busy patrolling the area. Lieutenant Gardner, Company M. Second Minnesota Cavalry, had gone on a five-day scouting mission with Gabriel Renville. Hostile Indians had been seen in the area, but none were seen by the soldiers. They returned to the post August 19, 1864.

In a letter to Robert Henry, Volga, South Dakota; Robert Holman, a former member of Company E., Thirtieth Wisconsin Infantry, recalled his memories of the establishment of Fort Wadsworth.

> ...I was in Co. "E" 30th Wis. Inf. Capt. Devlin, who was in the 2nd Wis. Reg., was our first Capt.-assigned Jan. 8, 1865 thro a Lt. from another Co. Darius D. Chappell was appointed our Capt. Capt. L. S. Burton was of Co. "B" same regiment. He died in, I think, St. Paul or Minneapolis taken sick on our way to Fort Snelling, Minn., where we started from to go to Dakota.
>
> Genl. Pope was in command of the Dept. of the North West with Hd. Quarters in Milwaukee, Wisc., after his defeat in the 2nd Battle of Bullrun. I was detailed in the spring of '63 to go to his Hd. Qtrs. as an orderly and was with him until, I think, June 1864, when that part of our Regt. there in Milwaukee was ordered to Dakota to build the fort with a Section of Artillery from Minn. and some Cav. I think there were about 1000 all told.
>
> We left Fort Snelling about July 4, 1864. It was very hot and dry, water very scarce in the western part of Minn. We dried up every well we came across. The lake water was not fit to drink—alkali. At places we had to march at night where we had 30 or more miles to the next watering place. Major Clowney was in command of the expedition. We had several good teams of mule and several ox teams. They suffered for water. One day we were marching along and the oxen began to sniff. There was no sign of water, but in a few minutes they stampeded and away they went on the run with their loaded wagons. No one could stop them. They went about 1 1/2 or 2 miles over a bank in a lake and when we got up to them they were all dead and the wagons out in the lake.
>
> We had to dig wells almost every night. I think we lost 15 or 18 oxen at that time. We went between Lake Traverse and, I think the other lake was called Big Stone Lake—it was near the line of Minnesota and Dakota. I think we went west about 75 miles and came to this chain of lakes—there were several of them and the land selected to build the Fort was surrounded by water. An inlet probably about 200 ft. wide. It was about 40 or 60 acres all told as near as I can remember, with good oak trees on the edges of all the Lakes, and some good cottonwood. We took up a Portable Saw Mill with us and a man to run it, hired by the Quartermaster. In

fact, he was his brother-in-law, a citizen drawing big wages. He was two or three days trying to get the frame together, and Bob, you know Mr. Clowney, was a Mechanic. He was a partner of my cousin, Richard Clark, and I used to work for them, and Mr. Clowney knew I understood drawings pretty well after working over 3 years at the Pattern-making trade in England.

So after watching this man for some time, he came to me and said, 'Jimmie, I want to detail you to put this sawmill together.' I looked at him and said, 'Major, I never saw a portable sawmill in my life.' 'Well,' he said, 'you understand drawings and you can do it.' Well, I was detailed and I looked the Drawings over and soon had it altogether. We had ten mules for power and was cutting out logs, all outdoors—rain and shine. When it rained, I would go with a pail to the Quartermaster and call for some whiskey, and get it, too, and without any exception it was the best, purest whiskey I ever drank. Drink it out of a tin cup and it kept us from getting colds.

There were about fifteen hundred Indians camped about 1 1/2 miles from our fort but we had no trouble. They kept away from us. They did not like our bake ovens that were made of clay and had stovepipes sticking up for draft. They acted very suspicious of them, and the noise when cutting logs. They kept away for quite awhile. These lakes were full of fish and I made a boat while there. It was about 20 ft. long. We had lots of buffalo meat while there. They were plenty and so were the wolves. They did surely howl at night and came up to the man standing picket duty so he could see his eyes, but had to stand ready to bayonet him, dare not shoot and alarm the camp.

I started this at 8:30. It is now 9:45 and time for bed and I will finish it tomorrow, Sunday morning. We did not finish building the fort, I think, it was in October 1864, and we were relieved by Minnesota troops or by southerners who had been taken prisoners and swore allegiance to the US, but did not want to fight against their own people, but would fight against the Indians. We were ordered South. We dreaded that march back to the States and snow storms overtook us before we got there. I knew several of the men you wrote about. Major John Clowney, I worked for him before and after the War. He was a good friend to me. He was in the Mexican War.

Tom Prestley was a Lt. in Co. B. of our Regt., later Capt. after Capt. Burton died. I also knew Gen'l Pope well. I was with him over a year in Milwaukee, Wisc. He commanded the Dept of the North West. Capt. John Klatt was of Co. "K" of our Regt. They were on our left in Regimental line. After I got the sawmill working, Capt. Devlin appointed me Corporal Sept. 1864. I was then 20 years old.

(For ease in reading, the letter was divided into paragraphs).

According to historian D. D. Parker, Lewis C. Paxson enlisted in Company G, Eighth Minnesota Infantry, August 1862, when the Minnesota Uprising began. A Pennsylvanian, he had traveled westward to Minnesota to teach. Two years later he and eight hundred other soldiers traveled across what is now Deuel and Day counties to the James River Valley and to Fort Rice on the Missouri River, south of present-day Bismarck, North Dakota.

That fall he and several others returned, passed through this area and spent a few days at the newly established Fort Wadsworth. The following excerpts are taken from his diary:

> Sat., Sept. 24, 1864: Marched 26 miles across a flat plain, which at first seemed only five miles wide (mirage). Camped near the head of the Coteau. Good Water. A horse tried to get up a bank and turned tumble set back into the water.

> Sun., Sept. 25, 1864: Hayes, Crow and myself went after plums and found only a few. Did not march today. Sent up rockets in the evening. Sermon, 'Beware, lest ye fall into like temptation.' I made a pair of mittens of socks, and took a general wash.

> Mon., Sept. 26, 1864: Marched 20 miles nearly south and reached Fort Wadsworth, D. T. afternoon. I bought five apple pies for $1. Gave one to Rigby, sold one to Everett, one to Knapp, one to Schaeffer; I lent 25 cents to Workman. Knapp paid for his pie. Rode Davis' horse.

> Tues., Sept. 27, 1864: Laid over Went after 'Return' to fort; paid 30 for rations; wrote to H. B. Grant. I lost and found pony. Cold and blustery.

> Wed., Sept. 28, 1864: I wrote to father. Very cold.

> Thurs., Sept. 29, 1864: Came 24 miles and encamped on very nice, large lake. Plenty of wood and grass.

Since the line of their march was leading toward the outlet of Big Stone Lake, the lake could have been Waubay, Enemy Swim or Pickerel Lake. On the next two nights, they camped on the Whetstone River. Then they crossed into Minnesota and camped on the LacQui Parle River on October 3rd when Paxson wrote: "We met Capt. Brackett's train enroute for Fort Wadsworth, 200 teams."

On September 28, 1864, Major Robert H. Rose with Companies B, C, D, and H of the Second Minnesota Cavalry assumed command of the spot. On October 17, he decided not to finish the buildings before winter since the logs were used up and no lumber was prepared for the quarters. The logs had to be cut on the opposite side of the lake and rafted across. Major Rose stated, "I hardly have the heart to ask a soldier (without extra pay) in this weather unless in cases of great emergencies as it is getting too late to do much carpenter work out-of-doors. We are too far north. So I have concluded it best to have the men fix up their temporary quarters as comfortably as possible..."

At this time, Major Rose decided the officers' quarters should be built of brick and stone. The buildings could be put up cheaper since there was an abundance of fieldstone and clay available.

Sisseton Indian women at Fort Wadsworth in 1864.
Photo courtesy South Dakota Historical Society - State Archives

In October 1864, Colonel Thomas and Company A, Second Minnesota Cavalry, stopped at Fort Wadsworth on their way from Fort Rice to Fort Snelling. One of the soldiers, Andrew Fisk, recorded the visit in his diary.

> Wed. 12. Camp No. 10 at Ft. Wadsworth. Arrived here about noon. Nice place, surrounded by numerous lakes, of fair water, and well timbered. Cos. B., C., D., and H. are here to winter. Capt. Davy stays here with his

H. Co., and Lt. Briley will go through with us. Saw Fred Marston, and lots of friends in the regiment. Getting ready to resume our march to the Minnesota frontier. I am to act as commissary. This is election day.

Thursday, Oct. 13. Ft. Wadsworth, D. T. Drew 12 days' rations. Boys got a half a sack of beans. Put the rations in Idaho wagons (some of the emigrants are returning with us from Ft. Rice to the States.) Took a walk with Fred. There is an Indian in the guard house, chained to a large rock. He has got so fat that he looks as though he would bust. Capt. Davy will go through with us.

Friday, Oct. 14. Camp No. 1. Left the Fort at 8 a.m. Made 15 miles. Camp on a small lake. Timber and grass. Traded horses with Capt. and put my horse in a team. Poor faithful John. He is nearly worn out. I doubt if he will see Ft. Ridgely. I shall give him a little grain and try and pull him through. Very windy and dusty. Met a large train of supplies going to Wadsworth. *Andrew Jackson Fisk Diary, January 1864-December 1866, from the Fisk Family Papers, Manuscript Collection 31, Montana Historical Society Archives, Helena, Montana.*

In November 1864, Company F, First United States Volunteers, arrived at Fort Wadsworth. Nicknamed the Galvanized Yankees or the Whitewashed Rebs, these Confederate prisoners were recruited from the Northern prison camps into the Union Army. They were required to take an oath of allegiance to the United States for their term of service. They helped with the building of the fort and were discharged from military service at the close of the Civil War.

In correspondence from Major Rose, dated November 1864, Lieutenant George W. Prescott (Aide-de-Camp and Acting Assistant Adjutant General) gave orders to bring the captive Indian Cho-we-tah-kah to trial at the post. He stressed taking every precaution against the escape of the prisoner and ordered to have him shot without hesitation if he tried. Also according to his orders: "The labor of preparing quarters, etc. will prevent for a time much attention to drill, but when time allows, that should be made a particular point and the most stringent discipline enforced among the troops under your immediate command. The company, United States Volunteers, will probably require supervision in both these respects."

Due to the shortage of hay, about one hundred horses were sent with Captain Raine to Fort Snelling, Minnesota, for the winter. This left thirty-two horses and seventy-eight mules at the fort for the first winter. (It took twenty-four mules to operate the saw mill daily). Grain for these animals was hauled in from Fort Ridgely, Minnesota.

The first winter at the fort was extremely difficult for the soldiers. They camped out in Sibley Tents until mid-November and then moved into hastily constructed cabins. The temporary shelters were damp, and most of the men suffered from colds, bronchitis and pneumonia. Because of the lack of fresh fruits and vegetables, many of the men also suffered from scurvy. Doctor B. P. Palmer, the fort doctor, ordered onions and vegetables to be issued to the troops twice a month. These were to be obtained from Fort Abercrombie. However, the two soldiers sent to Abercrombie for the vegetables returned with only 2/3 barrel of potatoes and one barrel of onions!

The daily schedule on March 1865 was as follows:

Daylight	Reveille	12 Noon	Dinner
6:30 a.m.	Breakfast	1:00 p.m.	Fatigue
7:30 a.m.	Fatigue	2:00 p.m.	Drill
8:00 a.m.	Sick Call	6:00 p.m.	Supper
9:00 a.m.	Guard Mount	Sunset	Retreat
10:00 a.m.	Drill	8:00 p.m.	Tattoo
11:45 a.m.	Orderlies	8:30 p.m.	Taps (lights Out)

During this time, four companies and a light artillery battery were stationed at Fort Wadsworth under the command of Major Robert Rose; Second Minnesota Cavalry, Companies B, C, D, and Company F of the United States Volunteers (Galvanized Yankees) and the Third Battery of the Minnesota Light Artillery.

The first winter at the fort introduced many of the men to blizzards on the Dakota prairies. An excerpt from a letter from Fort Wadsworth, Dakota Territory to the St. Paul Pioneer Press on April 8, 1865, provides an insight to a Dakota blizzard:

> We have just emerged from one of the severest snowstorms of the season. Not that a great deal of snow fell, but the drifting defies all power of description.
>
> From Monday morning until Wednesday afternoon the weather was mild, the wind from the southeast, with a heavy mist (and some rain) during that period. Wednesday evening the wind whipped suddenly to the northwest, and in an hour the snow was drifting furiously, and the cold increasing rapidly. By Thursday morning Boreas was on a regular bender, and continued his wild freaks until yesterday morning, when the drifting ceased, although the cold was severe during the day. This morning the wind is from the south, and the sun shines brightly, but the weather is raw and uncomfortable, and the immense snow drifts around the country gives the aspect of January much more than of April.

On Tuesday some families of Fort Thompson Sioux started for Oak Grove on the James River, and as the weather was then mild, they proposed taking the most direct route, regardless of the scarcity of timber on that route. There is a strong probability that some, if not all, of the party have frozen to death.

Some estimate may be formed of the severity of the storm, from the fact that although every possible exertion was made by the officers and employees of the Quartermaster's department for the preservation of the stock, one horse and four team mules were literally buried in the snow in the stable and around it. It was impossible to work facing the storm, and where men could work, there most strenuous efforts were insufficient to prevent the increase of the snow around them.

In the fort, communication was completely cut off between the different blocks of quarters. The messroom of the officers is not more than sixty or seventy yards from headquarters, yet the commanding officer got lost three times in his endeavor to keep up communication between the two!

Some of the small buildings occupied by the men in the fort were completely buried from sight, and every building was liberally supplied with snow through the roof and cracks in the plastering. The sutler's store that was intended to be made snowproof, was almost filled with snow from cellar to attic.

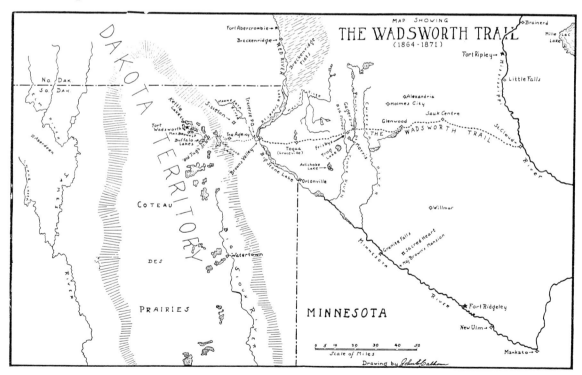

According to Grace Hall, author of *Wadsworth Trail*, supplies were shipped up the Mississippi River by boats to St. Cloud, MN and then transported by wagons on the Wadsworth Trail to Fort Wadsworth, Dakota Territory.

Reprinted from Wadsworth Trail with permission.

Although the soldiers were miles from the battles of the Civil War, they were kept informed of the situation. On April 4, 1865, a national salute of 100 guns was fired at Fort Wadsworth commemorating the capture of Richmond, Virginia (April 2). On April 9, General Robert E. Lee's army surrendered, and a 200-gun salute was fired at Fort Wadsworth on April 19.

During June 1865, Major Brown opened a mail route from Fort Wadsworth to Fort Ridgely, Minnesota. Previously, mail had been received from Fort Abercrombie. In September a post office was established at the fort with Jasper N. Searles as postmaster.

The first recorded Fourth of July celebration held in this area took place at Fort Wadsworth. According to the July 15th issue of the St. Paul Pioneer Press. The troops celebrated our country's 89th birthday in 1865 with much enthusiasm.

At ten in the morning the officers and troops assembled around the flag pole and listened while Captain J. N. Searles read the Declaration of Independence. Captain Everst was orator of the day. Lieutenant Weston fired the guns in salute to the thirty-six loyal states. Then a vocal group sang patriotic songs, some accompanied by a horn.

After dinner, the soldiers participated in a variety of races; one was a sack race; however, the greased pole event proved to be the most popular. The soldiers made a human pyramid to within a few feet of the top of the heavily greased pole. Then a 'Yankee Dutchman' climbed up the human pyramid and grasped the two five dollar bills in his hands!

The general and his staff from St. Paul usually made an annual inspection of the fort. They would be housed in the commanding officer's residence, and their visit was an excuse for social activities. General John M. Corse and his staff from Fort Snelling came to Fort Wadsworth on an inspection tour in the fall of 1865. Several officers, the soldiers and some of the scouts arranged a buffalo hunt for their distinguished guest. Led by Gabriel Renville, this group of a hundred men rode to a high peak in the Coteau about forty miles southwest of Fort Wadsworth, overlooking the James River flats. There they saw an immense herd of buffalo, estimated at 25,000 to 30,000 head.

Lieutenant David Inglis Scott, a native of England and one of General Corse's younger officers, had borrowed one of the swiftest and most valuable horses from the fort. Lieutenant Scott, a rather conceited fellow, was going to show the Indians how to shoot buffalo with a Colt revolver. Armed with several revolvers, he pointed out to the Indians that their long guns were useless. At a signal from Gabriel Renville, the Indians began yelling and creating such a disturbance that Scott became excited, dropped one of his pistols, and with the other accidentally shot his horse through the head!

Sam Brown, an experienced buffalo hunter, liked to single out the ugliest buffalo, drive it away from the herd, and then shoot it until it was dead. This time, Sam ran out of ammunition, and the huge beast chased him back to camp where Captain Mills came to his rescue and shot the buffalo.

A total of nearly three hundred buffalo were killed during that four-day hunt. Gabriel Renville killed sixteen, and Charles Crawford killed fourteen of the huge beasts. Most of the meat was given to the Indian people.

The hunters then organized a mythical Tatanka (Buffalo) Republic with Major Rose as president and Commander-in-chief, Major Joseph R. Brown as Secretary of War, Captain Arthur H. Mills as Quartermaster General, and Gabriel Renville as Captain General of the forces operating against the "Woolly Buffalo and the Wily Sioux."

Those were busy years at the fort. Emigrant trains from the East were required to stop at Fort Wadsworth to receive military inspection before moving out west. Often numerous smaller groups of emigrants traveled independently from the Minnesota area, sometimes within days of each other, with plans to rendezvous at Wadsworth. Here they rested, reorganized and united for their journey. They camped a mile east of the fort grounds.

Throughout 1865, the soldiers were busy building the fort. Material they used from April 1 to July 1865 included: 221,000 feet of lumber, 214 feet of shingles, 52,507 perch of stone, 215,000 bricks and 900 barrels of lime. The logs for lumber and shingles were found in the vicinity of the post, as were the rocks and sand for building and making lime. Carpenters, stone masons, brick layers, engineers and sawyers were hired to train the volunteer soldiers.

By the end of the year they had built the following:

    2 stone quarters for the men (45 ft. X 181 ft)
    1 stone stable (30 ft. X 200 ft.)
    2 board stables
    1 brick guardhouse (20 ft. X 50 ft.)
    1 warehouse (24 ft. X 145 ft.)
    1 hospital (40 ft. X 40 ft.) made of square timbers
    2 bastions
    1 magazine

1 carpenter shop
2 blacksmith shops (one for the quartermaster's work and one for the mounted companies)
1 wheelwright shop
1 good stone sawmill (enclosed and finished)
1 good brickyard in good order

The total cost of building the stone and brick buildings was estimated at two million dollars.

Andrew Jackson Fisk, the youngest brother of Captain James Fisk, the wagon train master, served as quartermaster sergeant of Company A, Second Minnesota Cavalry, at Fort Wadsworth from November 1865 to February 1866. Andrew, often referred to as "Jack," enlisted before his fifteenth birthday. He served under General Sully and was a member of the party that went to rescue his brother's wagon train in 1864.

According to Andrew's diary, dated October 25, 1865, his company was ordered to go to Fort Wadsworth. He said the men felt bad about going because it seemed "as though it was going out of the world again—but it is a soldiers duty to obey orders."

> Friday Nov. 3, 1865. Final orders rec'd to go to Wadsworth. The boys called a meeting and every one voted not to go. Capt. tried to argue us out of it, but to no avail. Gen. excitement. Rec'd letter from Bro. Jim and answered it.
>
> Sat. 4. Another meeting of co. tonight. Men again decided not to go to Wadsworth. Captain talked to us, and then Col. Phlander gave us a two hour talk. Then the men reconsidered the matter and decided to go. Taylor Knight, Shep and I have secured a good stove for our tent.

They left Fort Ridgely, Minnesota, on Sunday, November 5. During the next five days they marched about twenty to thirty miles a day. The weather was mild for November, but it felt good to have a stove at night.

> Friday Nov. 10. Camp on Big Stone Lake, near Lac Traverse. A slight shower this morning, but broke camp about 7 o'clock. Turned out to be a fair day. Made 22 miles. Had a fine view of Big Stone Lake. A stage station here, and 3 tepees of Indians. Not much wood but good water.
>
> Sat. 11. Camp at Dry Wood Lake, on the Coteau, Dacotah Ter. Made 18 miles. Comfortable marching, but wind blows hard tonight. Scenery

ground. (Scenic, ed.) At one point we could see both Big Stone Lake and Lake Traverse. We are now on the highest table land in the North American continent. Quite a bit of snow on the ground.

Sun. 12. Ft. Wadsworth D. T. Broke camp early. Capt. and I rode ahead and arrived 3 hours ahead of the company. The Fort has been greatly improved since we were here a year ago. Cos. H and K and the Battery are here. Stone quarters nearly completed for us to go into. Cummings arrived with a dispatch from Col. Phlander. Met many old friends and comrades. Letter from Fred [Marstrom].

Monday Nov. 13, 1865. Co. D. left for Ft. Snelling to be mustered out. Our men moved into their log huts until new quarters are completed. Taylor Knight, Jno. Smith, French, Dad and I in one hut. Busy all day getting straightened around. Sergt. Smith and 14 men detailed to take care of Co. horses. Also men detailed for the woods, and other duties.

Tu. 14. Took the best bath I could and put on some clean clothes-first time in nearly three weeks. Drew harness and got a Co. team in order. Putting up new stables and repairing the old ones. We indulged in a stag dance this evening. Weather warm.

Wed. 15. Capt. moved into his office and is all fixed up for the winter. Wrote to Bro. Jim, Ike Milner and Fred Marstrom. Another "stag" this evening.

Th. 16. Report today that Cos. A., B., F, & G. to be mustered out, and H., K., & L. to remain. Hope it is so. Wrote to Jack Milner. Cold and windy.

Fr. 17. Doc and Tom Holdship arrived from St. Paul via Ridgley. Doc looks well. Holdship has immense whiskers. Drew up a list of clothing needed by men.

Saturday Nov. 18, 1865. Drew and issued a large quantity of clothing. Warm Indian summer weather.

Sun. 19. A mail arrived from Ridgley. Was down to Co. K's quarters this evening. Considerable gambling going on there. Drew a regulation cap.

Mon. 20. Mail from Abercrombie. A Co. G man writes that Cos. A and G will be mustered out soon. Lyster bet Butterfield $5 that we would leave here before the 5th of Dec. Am going to Abercrombie with Lt. Briley.

Tu. 21. At a stockade, 38 miles from Wadsworth. Left at 9 a.m. Stopped at foot of Coteau and had a lunch. Splendid sight coming off the Coteau Forest fires in the Coteau. A detail of men from Co. B, H.I.M. Cav., garrison this stockade. A good set of boys. Ed Harkness and I sleep under the same blankets tonight.

Wednesday Nov. 22, 1865. Ft. Abercrombie, on Red River of the North. Arrived at 4 p.m. Saw Ike Milner, Marsh, Erve, and many other friends. Run across Capt. W.A.C. Ryan. Mighty glad to see him. He has been out trapping, and has developed into a splendid cook. Sleep with Ike tonight. Paymaster here. Lt. Briley lent me a "V". Has been a fine day.

Th. Nov. 23. Took a general survey of the fort today. Crossed the river and visited the store on that side. Lt. B. gave me an order for a canteen of whiskey, which I bought at that store. Stage in from St. Cloud. Bot some cheese and crackers for lunch going back. Start tomorrow.

F. 24. Twin Lakes. Left the fort at 8 and arrived here at 3. Very windy and disagreeable traveling. I am tanned up, brown as a berry. Am so tired that a blanket on the floor will be a luxury tonight.

Saturday, Nov. 25, 1865. Ft. Wadsworth. Arrived at 3 p.m. Received my pay, paid my debts, and have $20 left. Commenced bunking with Doc.

Sun. 26. Inspection. Doc and Shep up all night gambling. Wrote to Jack Milner. A. Blowers and P. Peterson each made $25 playing "Honest John."

Mon. 27. Four of Co. H men put in the guard house for refusing to drive mule team.

Tu. 28. Finished up the clothing rolls for the month. Doc off playing poker tonight.

Wed. 29. A large mail from Ridgley. Letters from Jack and Hettie. Wash for Captain all forenoon. Wind blows a hurricane.

Th. 30. Bet Tom Holdship an oyster supper that we would be out of the service by the 1st day of March, 1866. Cold tonight. It will freeze hard.

Fri. December 1, 1865. Bought a watch of C. Taylor. Gave $20 and a jacket. Went over to the Indian camp tonight. Traded my overcoat, blouse and an old blanket for a splendid buffalo robe.

Sat. 2. Boys are having great sport skating on the ice. Doc, Dad, Shep and Spillman playing poker all day. Shep is ahead.

Sun. 3. Inspection. Wrote to Hettie. Snowed 2 inches.

Mon. 4. Billy Goedert and Sport refused to go on the water wagon duty today and they had to pack cord wood. Men rushed out and cut them loose once. Captain took all the ammunition over to his office and read the army regulations to the men. Lt. Briley back from Abercrombie.

Tu. 5. This evening skated over to the Indian camp. Ice slick and clear from snow. J. Smith, A. Kleever, A. Bowman, A. Maxwell, S. Haydon, S. Pitcher and E. Leonard turned over the ordinance to me preparatory to going on a furlough.

Wed. 6. C. Spillman [Chas. J. Spillman, Co. A. age 23], E. Dexter [Eugene Dexter, Co. A, age 23] and Jack Young [Jacob Youngs, C. A, age 27] stole their horses out of the stable last night and deserted. Boys left on furlough. Considerable peach brandy circulating tonight. Jim Walker [Co. A Sergeant], Homer Hills [Co. A, Corporal] and I have 2 bottles. Rumored that the hay was going to be burned, and officers watched all night.

Thursday, Dec. 7, 1865. Thanksgiving Day. Nothing extra on our table. Was home a year ago today, and oh! how different. Major Rose called all the companies together today, gave them a talking to and much good advice. Capt. Howe made an ass of himself in his talk. There has been quite a spirit of unrest among the men. The men are anxious to return to civil life, and feel that favoritism has been shown in mustering out junior companies. Wrote to Jack Milner.

Fr., 8. A member of Co. H. [William M. Coles, Private, Co. K, age 23] died last night of typhoid fever. Curt Smith drunk as an owl. Several others are drinking. Lt. Briley [1st Lieutenant, Wm. L. Briley, age 25] gave me a song with music—"Wake Nickedemus the Slave."

Sat. 9. Capt. Field left for Abercrombie to attend a court martial. Co. K is turbulent today. Hooted one of their office[r]s. Several arrested but were afterwards released. A mail from Ridgley, but nothing for me.

Sun. 10. Inspection. Washed and changed clothes. Our boys caught many fish. They cut holes in the ice, and the fish bite greedily.

Monday, Dec. 11, 1865. Snowing for 24 hours and blowing a gale. Haven't been outdoors but twice today.

Tu., 12. Very cold—very. My pony broke through the ice while I was watering him and he nearly perished with cold before I could get him back to the stable.

Wed., 13. Bitter, bitter cold. Nearly froze my nose attending water call. At roll call Lieut. told the men to turn over to me tomorrow all their revolvers and spurs. Wrote to Fred Marston.

Th., 14. Men turned over revolvers and spurs. Alf. Bowman's discharge arrived, and also the application for Pop Winship's discharge. Wrote to Goody.

Fr. 15. Men turned in their sabre belts, and will carry their cap pouches and cartridge boxes on their carbine slings. Weather moderated a little.

Sat. 16. Men had a big time in the quarter last night. Beat drums and fired guns. Kept up the racket until 11 o'clock. All the noncommissioned officers were called over the Captain's office today and lectured.

Sun. 17. No inspection. Doc has a bad toothache. Snowed a couple inches.

Monday, Dec. 18, 1865. Akers has my robe done—had it lined. Was offered a good silver watch for it. A Co. H and a Co. K man had a set-to. Co. H won. Cold and windy.

Tu. 19. French has started a writing school, with 20 scholars. Bitter cold. Mail from Ridgley. Nothing for me.

Wed. 20. Commenced work on the rolls today—last muster for 1865. French and Lieut. are working on the clothing allowances of the men for the year. Thirty degrees below zero. No trouble to freeze yourself if you go outdoors.

Th., 21. Worked all day on the muster rolls. Not quite so cold. Mail due but has not arrived.

Fr. 22. Worked on rolls, and attended writing school tonight. Dame commenced to repair saddles.

Sat. 23. Boys killed one of the post hogs, and we will have a feast tomorrow. Weather has moderated.

Sunday, Dec. 24, 1865. Inspection in quarters this morning. Found that we were all right on carbines—full compliment. A fine breakfast on roast pig!

Mon. 25. A Merry Christmas, tho' it is rather a dull one for me. Was home a year ago, and at night attended a dance at Little Canada. Many of the men are celebrating by getting full of whiskey. A mail in from Abercrombie.

Tu. 26. Warm and pleasant. Played cards and read novels all day, and writing school this evening. A Ridgley mail has been due for several days. Must be a lot of letters for our company somewhere.

Wed. 27. Roast pig for breakfast, and writing school tonight. Storming and very windy.

Th. 28. Wrote all day on the muster rolls. Stage in, but no mail. Driver reports that one passenger froze to death [Adam Smith, Co. L, 2nd Cavalry], and another one, Ben. Franklin (both soldiers) whom I know, was frozen so badly that he will lose both legs and both arms.

Fr. 29. Still on muster rolls. Have had no mail from Ridgley for weeks.

Saturday, Dec 30, 1865. Finished up the pay and muster rolls. Some of the boys are drinking peach brandy pretty lively.

Sun. 31. An awful day—snowing and blowing furiously. Kept in the house and played seven-up. Mustered for pay this morning. This is the last day of 1865. One year ago was at Ft. Snelling in charge of the Convalescent Detachment. These pages record a good many incidents in many places. Good bye old year. In closing my second year's diary since I have been in the service, the thought arises—where will I be, and under what circumstances will I write of the closing days of 1866.

A year later on the Fisk Expedition to Montana Andrew penned this item in his diary for Monday, December 31, 1866.

But I must bid the old year "good bye". I cannot help—when looking over this book to think of the good times—bad times—happy times & Sad time—I have had during the past year. How well I remember one short year ago to night—how we boys sat around the warm stove at Ft. Wadsworth, D. T. & smoked our pipes—saw the old year out & the new one in—how I thought & wondered then where I would be one year from that time. But my diary for 1866 is full—so old year—farewell. *Andrew Jackson Fisk Diary, 1864-1866, from the Fisk Family Papers, Manuscript Collection 31, Montana Historical Society Archives, Helena, Montana.*

Andrew was in the service until his discharge in the spring of 1866. He and his brothers went to Montana, purchased a printing plant and started the Helena Herald newspaper. He was appointed postmaster in 1898.

Flatiron Reservation

On April 22, 1867, twenty-three representatives of the Sisseton-Wahpeton tribes, headed by Chief Gabriel Renville and John Other Day, signed a treaty which established the Flatiron Reservation. This triangular reservation stretched from the head of Lake Traverse southwest to Lake Kampeska, north to Lake Teuwakan then to the foot of Lake Traverse. The 918,779.32 acres of land lies mostly in present-day Roberts County and included farmland, lakes for fish and waterfowl and many acres of trees; 4480 acres of land was sliced off the eastern side of Fort Wadsworth Military Reservation for the new reservation.

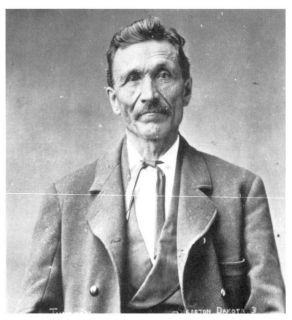

Gabriel Renville (Ti Wakan, which means Sacred of Holy Lodge). Gabriel was born on the east side of Big Stone Lake in 1825 and died at Sam Brown's cabin in Browns Valley, MN, in 1892. He spoke no English but was a master of the Sioux language. He was elected chief of the Sisseton-Wahpeton Indians after the death of Red Iron in 1884.

Minnesota Historical Society.

This reservation, also known as the Sisseton-Wahpeton Indian Reservation or the Lake Traverse Reservation, was established for the Indians who helped the United States during the Minnesota Uprising of 1862 and continued their service by keeping the hostiles from raiding the frontier. Friendly Indians from other tribes were also allowed on the new reservation.

During 1869, the reservation was surveyed according to the terms of the treaty of February 19, 1867, which stated that the land be apportioned into 160 acre tracts to the head of a family or any single person over twenty-one years of age who wanted to cultivate the soil and live on it. The land was also divided into forty-acre tracts.

The Indians set up a government and organized it into ten districts. Their constitution and bylaws were approved by the Bureau of Indian Affairs. Gabriel Renville was elected chief for life and was paid four hundred dollars a year. The Indians lived in log or frame houses on farms scattered throughout the reservation. The Indian Agency was set up south of present-day Sisseton, South Dakota.

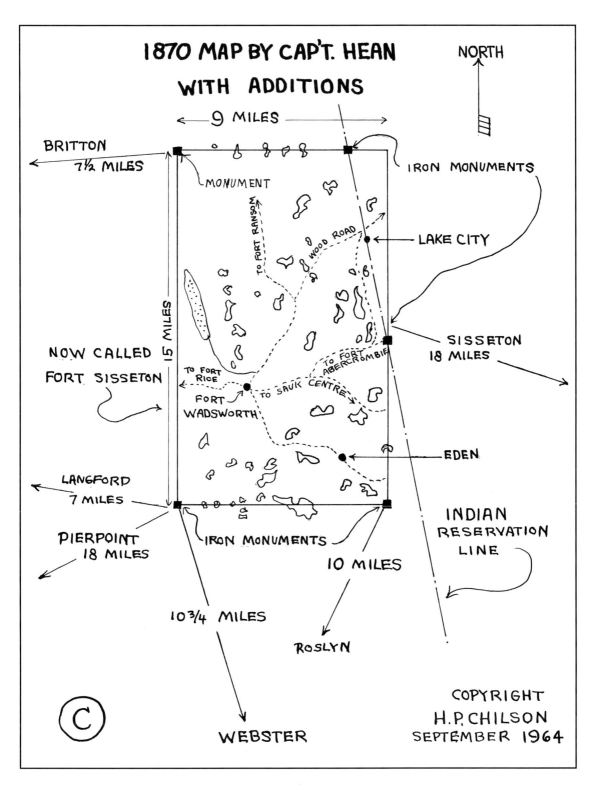

1870 MAP BY CAP'T. HEAN
WITH ADDITIONS

NORTH

← 9 MILES →

BRITTON
7½ MILES

IRON MONUMENTS

MONUMENT

TO FORT RANSOM

WOOD ROAD

LAKE CITY

15 MILES

NOW CALLED
FORT SISSETON

TO FORT RICE

TO FORT ABERCROMBIE

SISSETON
18 MILES

FORT
WADSWORTH

TO SAUK CENTRE

EDEN

LANGFORD
7 MILES

INDIAN
RESERVATION
LINE

PIERPOINT
18 MILES

IRON MONUMENTS

10 MILES

10¾ MILES

ROSLYN

Ⓒ

WEBSTER

COPYRIGHT
H. P. CHILSON
SEPTEMBER 1964

A second reservation was set up in the Devils Lake area, now known as Fort Totten, North Dakota. Other members of the Sisseton-Wahpetons and the Cuthead band of the Yanktonais settled there. Little Fish was their chief.

During the fall of 1873, Major J. E. Yard's report revealed that two bands of peaceful Sisseton-Wahpeton Indians, (eight hundred to a thousand) lived on the Sisseton-Wahpeton Indian Reservation adjoining the military reservation. To some extent they were supported by the government. The government furnished them with cattle and farming implements. They were paid for the work they did with food and clothing. Most built houses and had cattle, horses, pigs and chickens. Some adopted the white man's style of clothing. Several had shotguns, and a few owned revolvers. As a general rule, they had to receive permission from their agent, Moses Adams, to leave the reservation.

In the Waubay area, there were between forty to fifty Yanktonai Indians living on the reservation. They received no aid from the government.

Chapter Four

Living Conditions at the Fort

*"I have talked with these Indians kindly, because it is a duty
to do everything possible to prevent trouble or bloodshed."*
Captain Clarence E. Bennett
March 17, 1880

Life in the barracks was not always comfortable or sanitary. According to military reports it was deemed unhealthy to have the living quarters and eating facilities under the same roof. Each of the two stone barracks housed the sergeant's quarters, mess hall, washroom, kitchen and sleeping areas for the enlisted men. Each company had a kitchen but no regularly assigned cook. Privates were assigned the task of cooking for their company and baking bread in the bake house (another building) for a period of ten days at a time.

The soldiers built their narrow wooden bunks. Two men slept on the top bunk, and two men slept on the bottom bunk. They slept "head to toe", meaning each soldier faced his bunkmate's feet. This was for sanitary reasons, so that no one breathed in another's face. Each bunk was supplied with two wool blankets and a straw tick mattress which had to be refilled with fresh straw or hay every month or so. Pillows were not government issue, so if a soldier wanted something under his head, he wadded up some of his clothing. Metal single cots were issued on June 8, 1873.

Order No. 207, issued December 17, 1882, stated, "The whole bedding of enlisted men will when ordered, be put out and thoroughly aired, blankets opened and well shaken. Any soldier neglecting or refusing will immediately be confined to the Guard House." And the records reveal that this did happen!

Bedbugs caused problems numerous times in the barracks, the guard house and the officers' quarters. In July 1879, Captain Bennett issued an order to get rid of all the swallows and their nests immediately. He stated, "One wall of my house is covered with bedbugs in such numbers as I never saw in officers' quarters before. The swallows' nests were covered with bedbugs."

Captain Bennett reported the incident to the Adjutant General in Fort Snelling, Minnesota. "I have tried at my quarters, scalding water, Scalding brine, fumes of sulphur, Salt, Ovail Oil, white washing and lime paste and the family [wife, children and two maids] is employed nightly burning them from the walls with the flames of lighted candles, we have killed over a thousand a night in the last three nights. The buildings are of brick and mortar cracked. They are between the bricks and around the woodwork. Some of the public buildings are infested with bedbugs in immense numbers. The Commanding Officer's Quarters, now occupied by myself, and the Guard House swarm with them..."

Washing facilities for the soldiers were minimal. During the summer months, they bathed in the lakes. The washroom, adjacent to the mess hall, was used for shaving, washing mess kits and washing clothes. Bathhouses weren't constructed until 1883 for the company quarters. These bathing facilities were built in the rear of the quarters.

Barber chairs were set up in the washrooms. The post barber shop rates in 1877 were as follows: for officer, haircuts were $.20 or $1.25 a month, and shaves cost $.15; for enlisted men, haircuts were $.75 a month and shaves cost $.10.

Each company was allowed one tailor and four laundresses (later reduced to two) who were transported to the new post with the equipment. Laundress positions were usually allotted to the wives of senior non-commissioned officers. They drew rations like the soldiers; housing and fuel were furnished, as well as transportation to and from the fort. Like the soldiers, they were subject to military discipline.

Laundresses could earn up to thirty or forty dollars a month. They were allowed to charge one dollar a month for washing a soldier's clothes. Laundresses lived in the small one-story log cabins abandoned by the officers when they moved into their new brick buildings. These cabins were located south of the

These log cabins, located south of the south barracks, were built for the officers in 1864. When the officers moved into their new brick structures, these nine log cabins were turned over to the laundresses. This area became known as 'Suds Row,' or 'Soap Suds Row'.

South Dakota Game, Fish & Parks. Originally housed at National Archives.

south barracks in an area known as "Suds Row," or "Soap Suds Row." In 1868, two laundresses, Betty Rencer and Louisa Roi, both died of consumption within a week of each other. By 1874, records reveal eight laundresses, including the hospital matron, at the fort.

The army banned the enrollment of laundresses in 1878, but a laundress could continue working until her husband's enlistment period ended. Laundresses were still employed at Fort Sisseton until the early part of 1883.

Soldiers wore Civil War uniforms, wool in the winter and cotton in the summer. It wasn't until 1873 that the soldiers were issued warm winter clothing, woolen mittens, buffalo overshoes and lined overcoats. Previous to this time, soldiers either purchased or traded articles of clothing at the sutler's store. Even after the uniforms were made according to the new revised sizes, the soldiers still had to have alterations done at their expense by the tailors at the fort.

Soldiers were issued .55 caliber muskets; troopers had the long triangular bayonets, while the cavalry had the curved sabor. Officers were armed with revolvers and curved swords.

Although the fort was surrounded by small bodies of water, finding good drinking water was always a challenge. Drinking water was obtained from nearby springs and lakes and hauled in water wagons by four mules. Because

71

This log structure is similar to the seventy-six by twenty-one foot building that stood east of the guardhouse. According to Marvin Scott's *History of Fort Sisseton*, a building similar to this one was shown on the von Minden sketch as a "loghouse used for Officers and Officers' quarters." It was divided between the chapel and the saddler's shop in 1871. Three fifths of the building on the west became the saddler's shop while two fifths of the building on the east became the chapel. Notice the cross on the building to the left.

Roy P. Johnson Collection. Assumption Abbey Archives.

of the alkaline qualities, the water in the lake was unfit for drinking or cooking, yet the cattle thrived on it. The army had never been able to obtain good drinking water at the fort by digging wells, so they were always on the lookout for new methods. Eleven galvanized sheet iron cisterns that held 200 barrels of water each were installed in October 1871 to catch and hold rainwater. Additional cisterns were added in 1878 when two companies of soldiers were again stationed at the fort.

According to Captain Bennett, water in the lakes had fallen twelve feet the first twelve years of the fort's existence. The water in some of the lakes and sloughs dried up, and others were very low. In planning for the future, the army considered using a team force pump to bring water from Clear Lake, nine miles away.

The ice storage houses by the lakes were filled every winter. The first thatched roof icehouse was replaced with a log building large enough to hold 700 tons of ice. Ice was melted for drinking during the summer months, when lake water was unfit to drink.

A twelve months' supply of food staples was usually kept on hand. Beef was purchased on contract, kept and butchered as needed. In 1878, a slaughter house was built, and orders were issued regarding the care, feeding, watering and sheltering of the cattle. The result was much better quality beef. First Lieutenant J. M. Burns of the 17th Infantry issued the following rules on October 19, 1878:

The following rules will be observed by the Non. Com. Officers in charge at the Beef Herd, who will be held responsible for a strict compliance therewith. Viz:

- The cattle will be watered regularly twice each day. Morning and evening.
- During suitable weather the cattle will be turned out to graze at daylight, and returned to the corral at sunset, each day, and in no case will any of the cattle be driven to the corral without water.
- They will be counted each evening by the Non-Commissioned officer in charge, when returned to the corral for the night and if any of the cattle are absent, he will report at once to the A.A.S.C. [Assistant Adjutant Commissary Sergeant].
- The cattle ordered corn-fed will be kept tied in stalls, regularly watered and fed corn twice a day and hay three times a day, in such amounts as shall be ordered from time to time by the A.A.C.S. They must be kept clean, and the stall cleaned daily.
- In bad weather the balance of herd will be tied in the stable and fed hay twice a day.
- In fair weather when there is no grazing, they will be turned loose in the yard and fed there.
- The stable must be kept clean.
- All the cattle will be salted once a week. Salt to be drawn from the Commissary for this purpose.

A small flock of sheep was also kept on the fort grounds. While the cattle were housed two hundred yards from the garrison, the hogs had to be at least four hundred yards from the fort.

During the first years, there were no gardens in or near the fort, so canned goods were sold to officers and companies. Later, the soldiers planted three vegetable gardens a half-mile south of the fort complex. One garden was for the officers (two acres), one for the hospital use (seven acres), and one for the enlisted men.

Homesteaders like George Bryant of Andover had heard of the huge gardens raised by the soldiers at the fort. In 1882, he wrote to Captain Bennett asking for information about the yield and growth of crops in the area. Bennett replied that the past season Companies F and I, 17th U. S. Infantry, the post hospital and the post trader all had fine gardens. The following were raised in the company gardens: asparagus, corn, cucumbers, horseradish, lettuce, watermelons, muskmelons, onions, parsnips, pumpkins, potatoes, peas, peppers, radishes, rhubarb, squash, turnips, tomatoes, caraway, dill and sage.

To store the garden produce, two root cellars were built in 1882 for the two companies. Sergeant Robert White and ten soldiers were sent thirteen miles from the fort to cut wood for the posts and beams in the root cellars. Both cellars were forty-four feet long by twenty-two feet wide. The roof rested on heavy oak posts, and the walls were planked over and covered with clay. The chimney was placed in the center between the two cellars so produce could be placed in each storage bin. At the west end of the company cellar there was a fourteen by twenty-two foot cellar for the officers' use.

During July 1873, a hail storm destroyed their gardens. Some years grasshoppers and drought reduced the anticipated yield.

Dogs at the fort often destroyed gardens and caused other problems. It got to the point that those who wished to keep dogs had to make out a written application, and all unauthorized dogs were destroyed. In 1877, the list of authorized dogs numbered seventeen, most of them retrievers and spaniels belonging to the officers.

Apparently, certain dogs had the irritating habit of howling at the sound of the bugle at reveille and retreat. The scouts were ordered to drive the guilty dogs out of the garrison, follow them and shoot them.

The sheepherder was given permission to shoot dogs found killing sheep belonging to the post. In one incident, the greyhounds were chasing the mules and the cattle and barking at the aides, children, laundresses, and servants. Those dogs were ordered to be whipped, and the owners were to take measures to stop the complaints.

One can easily read the names carved in the bricks of the guardhouse. Soldiers who had to spend time in jail were allowed one hour of fresh air daily. While they soaked in the sunshine or shivered in the cold air, some spent time carving their names in the bricks.

Johnson Photo Collection

Soldiers from Fort Wadsworth were sometimes called upon to settle disputes and make arrests outside the military reservation. In December 1873, Mr. Moses N. Adams, Indian Agent at the Sisseton Indian Agency, requested assistance from the commander at Fort Wadsworth. Major R. E. A. Crofton sent Lieutenant Frank D. Garretty of the 17th Infantry and thirty-two soldiers to the agency on the 16th to stop a disturbance. Agent

74

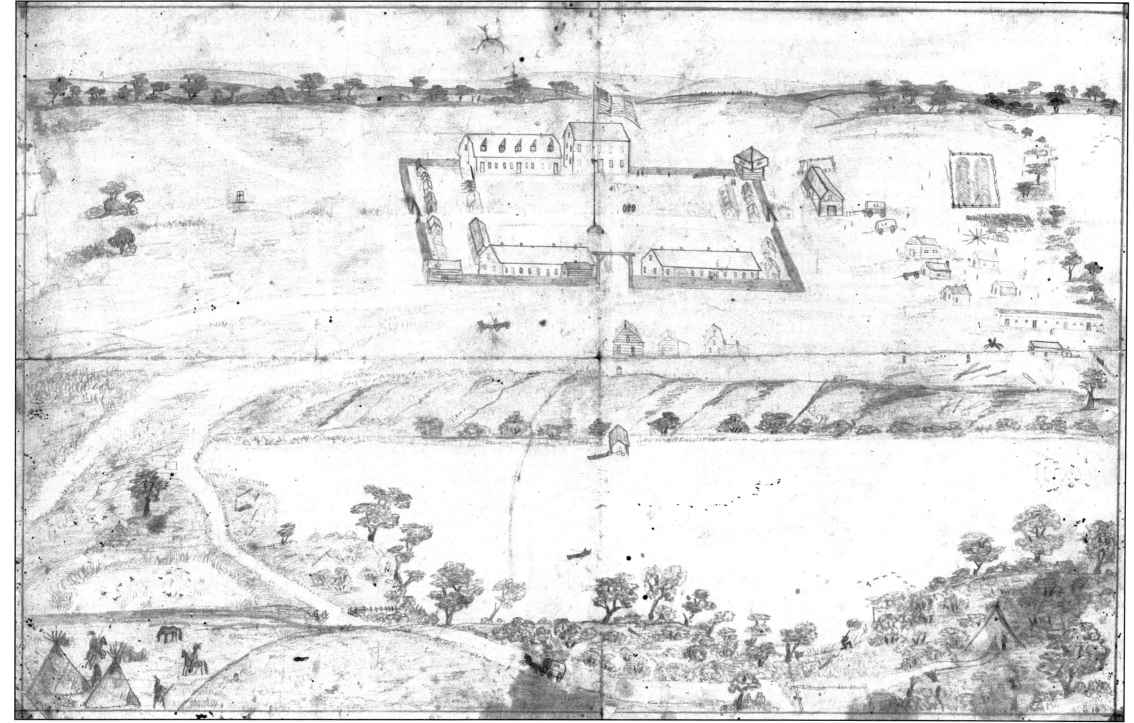

Maximilian Miller sketched this drawing of Fort Wadsworth, Dakota Territory. Miller was born in Baden, Germany. He was nineteen years old when, as a volunteer, he enlisted on December 2, 1865, in Philadelphia, PA. He re-enlisted in the 10th US Infantry Company C at Fort Wadsworth, Dakota Territory, on December 2, 1868, for a three-year period. He spent thirty-four years in military service.

Chilson Photo Collection.

Adams arrested two Indian leaders, Two Stars and Good Boy. They (Two Stars and Good Boy) had taken away the cattle and wagons issued to Thomas Robertson, Angus Robertson and David Grey Cloud and returned them to the Indian agency. They demanded that the cattle and wagons be re-issued to members of the tribe, not half-breeds. The two men went peacefully with the Lieutenant and his men to Fort Wadsworth and were placed in confinement in the guardhouse. Nine soldiers were left at the agency to assist in keeping things under control. On January 26, 1874, the two men were released from the guardhouse.

Once the initial building projects were completed, the parade grounds were used nearly every day for drill. In the 1880s, numerous repairs were made to the buildings, gravel walks were laid out, weeds were cut, drains were cleared, some new drains were put in and roads were graveled by the officers' and companys' quarters. In 1885, the gravel walks were replaced with 854 feet of boardwalk. In 1887, twenty pounds of Kentucky blue grass seed and thirty pounds of white clover were sown on the parade grounds.

The soldiers built a 185-foot x 8-foot porch on the north barracks in 1885.
South Dakota Game, Fish & Parks. Donated by Karl J. Vander Horck.

Pressure was brought to bear on Congress to rename Fort Richmond on Staten Island, New York, in General Wadsworth's honor. Consequently, the name of Fort Wadsworth was changed to Fort Sisseton by General Order number ninety-four on August 29, 1876 in honor of the Sisseton band of the Sioux Indians.

Since the fort was located too far from any town, recreational activities centered in and around the fort. These included fishing, ice skating, hunting and swimming in the surrounding lakes. According to Sam Brown's diary, a tragedy occurred May 30, 1865, when five soldiers went swimming. One of the swimmers, Roy Anderson from Company B, drowned.

Soldiers went fishing and hunting for pleasure and often returned with fish or fowl to supplement their diet. Apparently, they killed plenty of prairie chickens because on December 2, 1876, an order was issued to prohibit the killing of those birds on the Military Reservation. This order constituted the first known conservation proclamation for this area.

According to the *Reporter and Farmer,* the Webster newspaper, the soldiers at Fort Sisseton organized a baseball team and played against the Webster Pastime Baseball Club. The first game was played on the fort grounds in August, 1888. Several men and women accompanied the team to the fort and all were entertained royally by the soldiers. They prepared a dinner for their guests and they gave them a tour of the library, school room, hospital, and stables until the game started. The game lasted two hours with Webster winning with a score of fifteen to twelve.

After the game, the Webster ladies presided at the organ, and all joined in singing gospel hymns. A soldier accompanied with his guitar. Company A exhibited its military drill. The soldiers then served lunch.

Indoors, the soldiers were apt to spend their free time gambling, playing cards, dancing (stag), loafing or drinking peach brandy. According to Andrew Fisk's diary, Corporal French had a writing school for the men a couple nights a week. On December 14, 1870, the soldiers put on a melodrama in three parts in their post theater that they called, "Theatre Comique Wadsworth". The play, "The Idiot Witness", a tale of blood by J. T. Hanes, was followed by "State Secrets", and concluded with the laughable farce "Paddy Miles's Boy."

The Post Traders Store, east of the north barracks, had clubrooms set aside, one each for the enlisted men and the officers. Enlisted men also held parties and dances in their quarters. The following invitation is on display in the Fort Sisseton Visitor Center:

Fort Wadsworth, D. T.
Dec. 23, 1867

The Misses Brown,
Are respectfully invited to attend a Ball and Supper to be given by Company C,
10th Infantry in their quarters on Christmas evening December 25, 1867.

Dancing commences at 8 p.m.
Supper———————midnight

Fergus I. C. Bentley
1st Sergt. Sev. C 10th Inf.
on behalf of the Company

One of the Brown ladies, Ellen Brown, met her future husband, John Sylvanus Allanson, at one of these social functions. They were married December 28, 1869. The ladies were the daughters of Major Joseph Brown.

An item from the Saint Paul Pioneer Press on September 6, 1864, describes the plight of the Wadsworth soldiers in the earlier days.

> Old Books for Soldiers—Five companies of gallant Minnesota soldiers, who would rather be fighting rebels are cooped up in the heart of the western wilderness, 300 miles west of S. Paul, and nearly 200 miles beyond our furthest western frontier. In this idle solitude time hangs heavy on their hands. But their greatest privation is the want of something to read. They appeal to the Ladies Sanitary Branch to send them books, pamphlets, magazines, newspapers, anything to while away the tedious time.
>
> The attention of all who sympathize with the soldiers' needs is directed to this appeal. All who have old books, magazines, or newspapers which they wish to donate to the soldiers at Fort Wadsworth are requested to send them to the Capitol tomorrow (Wednesday) morning.
>
> By the Secretary

In 1867, a design for a chapel and school had been submitted to General Grant and revoked. Grant was of the opinion that the post was temporary and not entitled to funding from an Act of Congress, July 28, 1866. It was deemed wiser and more expedient to spend monies for providing comfortable quarters for the troops and for effectively guarding and protecting public supplies. However, in 1869, a log structure for a chapel and a school was erected.

In 1870, there were ninety-four volumes in the library, and in 1875 Dr. Knickerbocker reported the post library had two hundred volumes, but it is not known where the library was located at that time.

A new brick building (twenty feet x thirty feet) housing a library and a school was completed in 1881. That was the year it became mandatory to have school at army posts. The plan for this brick structure was approved June 5, 1880, at a cost of $374.99. The schoolroom occupied the west wing; a court martial room and chapel, the east wing; the library and meeting room, the center. Records reveal that there were between seven and fifteen elementary age children in school. School started at 8:30, but in the winter it began at 9 a.m. If a teacher was drawn from the post (an enlisted man), he would be paid an extra $.35 a day. Otherwise, a civilian teacher would be hired.

In 1880, the post library was closed every Wednesday evening so the Sisseton Lodge of the Good Templars (temperance lodge) could hold its meetings. Enlisted men who were members were excused from retreat and roll call every Wednesday.

The fort band was active nearly every year. Musicians were paid extra wages and were ordered to practice two hours each day. In 1874, the Seventeenth Regiment Band of the United States Infantry from Fort Abercrombie, Dakota Territory, arrived at the fort for a two weeks' stay to entertain the troops at Wadsworth. The Fort Sisseton String Band performed in Webster the afternoon and evening of July 4th, 1884.

Since the fort was located so far from civilization, a medical officer had to be stationed at the post. If one was not available from the army, a civilian doctor had to be hired on a monthly salary. On May 14, 1868, the Surgeon General's Office in Washington, D.C. adopted a new hospital record book which included a special section for zoology. Therefore, after this time, the fort doctor would have to record the names of all the birds, animals, and plants which they observed, as well as keeping vital statistics. Assistant Surgeon General Doctor Knickerbocker arrived at the fort on November 6, 1868, and recorded his observations sporadically throughout late 1868 and all of 1869. On foot and

The first hospital, built of hewed logs, was replaced by this story-and-a-half brick structure in 1868. Equipment for recording weather data is on the left.

South Dakota Game, Fish & Parks. Donated by Karl J. Vander Horck.

79

Knickerbocker's list of animals included the following:

elk	buffalo	large gray wolf
black bear	otter	marten deer
red fox	badger	skunk
weasel	beaver	rabbit
muskrat	Richardson ground squirrel	Franklin ground squirrel
antelope		

His list of birds during 1869 included the following:

common loon	red-necked grebe	white pelican
brant	trumpeter swan	white-footed goose
gadwall	pintah	green-winged teal
blue-winged teal	wood duck	bufflehead
common merganser	turkey vulture	Mississippi kit
rough-legged hawk	bald eagle	sparrow hawk
killdeer	sandhill crane	common gallinule
woodcock	coot	common snipe
long-billed curlew	American avocet	rock dove
ring-billed dove	screech owl	snowy owl
chimney swift	downy woodpecker	barn swallow
blue jay	crow	common gackle
wood thrush	Northern shrike	robin
red-winged blackbird	western meadowlark	snow bunting
greater-prairie chicken	goshawk	

and by horseback, he roamed over the entire Military Reservation. He, like his successor, Doctor McChesney in 1869, probably traveled between twenty and thirty miles from the fort on these observation trips.

In 1874, the medical officer sent two ducks to the Smithsonian Institute for identification. (This was one of the ways frontier doctors were instructed to obtain correct identification of the birds.) The report stated that they were an adult female and a young male canvasback, the same type duck that was found in the Chesapeake Bay area in the northeastern part of the United States.

Since wild rice was a favorite food of all the ducks, particularly the mallards, Captain E. Bennett requested wild rice seed sent out to the fort. The seed arrived from the Commissioner of Agriculture in Washington, D.C. Captain Bennett and his men sowed the wild rice in the nearby lakes, since wild rice thrives in soft, deep mud and shallow, moving water. He had Mr. Cusins plant the rice seeds around the edges of Lake Wahbay. Then he gave some to the Indian Agent Charles Crissy at the Sisseton Agency to plant on the reservation and to George J. Becker, a farmer, to plant at the head of Big Stone Lake. Apparently, the seeds were too old, because nothing grew in any of these places.

Captain Bennett became impatient to get a crop started, so he wrote again in 1883, requesting six bushels of wild rice from last year's growth to plant in the vicinity of the fort. Again nothing grew.

Even though the new brick hospital was completed in December 1868, numerous problems surfaced during the next few years. The barracks and the hospital were heated by iron box stoves which would have produced enough heat if sufficient fuel could have been obtained. Hospital patients suffered severely. Since it was impossible to heat the whole room, the beds were often moved close to the stove. Some time later, orders wcrc issued stating that when the hospital was occupied by the sick, the hospital should be the first to receive the daily supply of wood.

At times, disagreements arose between the commanding officers and the medical staff. For example, the commanding officers once required the hospital cook and nurse to attend the drills and room orderly duties of their company; thus leaving the hospital without adequate supervision. There were particularly strong disagreements between Dr. Knickerbocker and the post commander, who said in his reports, "Patients suffered inconveniences and that no actual suffering was caused." However, Doctor Knickerbocker's reports indicate something more serious. One report told about James Palmer, a

Monthly Absolute Minimum Temperatures

(With Monthly and Annual Averages)

	Jan	Feb	Mar	April	May	June	July	Aug	Sept	Oct	Nov	Dec	Annual
1867	-27	-24	-24	7	30	48	57	----	36	24	4	---	-------
1868	-12	---	---	---	---	---	---	---	---	---	---	---	-------
1869	---	-19	-24	21	35	42	53	55	31	5	-5	-17	-------
1870	-25	-30	-19	9	39	42	54	40	41	22	11	-28	13
1871	-24	-23	2	18	34	49	51	49	34	16	-24	-30	13
1872	-29	-26	-20	4	29	41	43	44	29	15	-20	-35	8
1873	-32	-32	-22	15	28	48	47	48	22	-9	-7	-23	6
1874	-28	-25	-12	4	31	37	46	51	32	6	-11	-23	9
1875	-37	-33	-18	5	22	31	48	45	28	5	-25	-22	4
1876	-27	-20	-18	14	24	34	40	32	19	10	---	-28	-------
1877	-29	-10	-15	6	30	---	---	42	---	---	---	---	-------
1878	-25	---	9	25	30	45	51	---	---	8	---	-25	-------
1879	-34	-32	-21	3	33	---	49	---	---	6	-8	-40	-------
1880	-24	-16	-20	---	---	40	45	41	27	9	-20	-45	-------
1881	-32	---	-9	-2	26	46	51	48	30	20	-15	-11	-------
1882	-26	-23	-14	6	25	37	49	41	28	17	-7	-30	9
1883	-41	-38	-19	15	25	35	40	40	19	15	-15	-27	4
1884	-44	-29	-23	16	27	44	44	41	32	12	-22	-38	5
1885	-37	-36	-16	11	20	32	40	33	27	12	5	-19	6
1886	-44	-36	-12	4	28	36	50	29	17	19	-17	-37	3
1887	-40	-38	-2	2	27	33	41	33	28	-6	-24	-30	2
1888	-38	-35	-15	2	14	39	49	40	32	24	4	-3	9
1889	-25	-30	-3	17	---	---	---	---	---	---	---	---	-------
Means	-31	-28	-14	10	28	40	47	42	28	11	-11	-27	8

Frontier fort doctors also recorded and compiled vital weather statistics.

Monthly and Annual Precipitation

(In Inches)

	Jan	Feb	Mar	April	May	June	July	Aug	Sept	Oct	Nov	Dec	Annual
1866	---	---	---	---	---	---	---	---	0.23	---	---	---	---
1867	---	---	---	---	7.96	13.8	8.88	2.37	1.65	---	---	---	---
1869	0.20	1.47	0.49	1.82	1.54	0.99	0.67	3.31	2.76	0.41	0.36	0.07	14.09
1870	0.48	0.25	0.67	0.23	5.51	4.73	2.63	0.89	0.45	1.50	0.20	0.32	17.86
1871	0.44	0.30	1.08	2.36	0.74	1.96	1.48	0.76	0.36	0.60	0.52	0.20	10.80
1872	0.20	0.22	0.64	1.78	4.38	4.02	5.04	2.56	1.34	2.46	0.56	0.16	23.36
1873	2.14	1.16	1.22	2.54	4.52	2.82	3.82	2.00	1.10	3.26	1.16	1.38	27.12
1874	1.18	2.40	3.90	1.84	2.70	4.56	1.16	3.34	0.62	3.90	2.60	4.24	32.44
1875	2.84	6.30	4.50	2.78	3.06	2.22	2.70	4.16	2.04	0.36	0.30	0.14	31.40
1876	0.88	0.54	0.80	1.92	1.46	1.52	2.00	4.86	2.22	1.84	---	0.82	---
1877	0.66	0.00	1.22	1.74	---	---	---	0.80	---	---	---	---	---
1878	0.14	---	2.04	5.00	2.00	3.50	4.70	---	---	0.50	---	0.74	---
1879	0.08	0.80	0.34	1.50	4.50	---	6.76	---	1.20	0.80	0.00	0.80	---
1880	0.30	0.22	2.00	---	3.50	6.00	5.08	3.88	0.60	2.26	0.12	0.20	---
1881	0.56	---	2.00	1.30	2.52	2.86	1.02	3.96	1.64	1.62	0.26	0.12	---
1882	0.36	0.32	1.04	2.46	2.20	7.42	3.64	1.02	0.36	3.50	0.70	0.19	23.21
1883	0.13	0.22	0.05	1.12	2.51	1.08	2.22	1.92	1.65	2.07	---	0.35	---
1884	0.35	0.82	0.82	1.26	3.00	1.32	3.45	2.37	1.43	3.63	0.52	1.31	20.28
1885	0.48	0.15	0.40	1.86	1.79	3.74	2.79	1.53	4.10	0.70	1.70	0.75	19.99
1886	0.60	0.65	0.55	3.06	1.64	1.72	1.23	1.60	0.78	1.00	0.96	0.32	14.11
1887	0.40	0.46	0.42	2.80	1.87	5.82	5.50	8.07	1.02	0.94	0.19	1.37	28.86
1888	0.25	0.17	0.59	0.60	1.90	1.56	3.48	2.10	0.08	0.60	---	0.08	---
1889	0.46	0.31	---	1.52	---	---	---	---	---	---	---	---	---
Means	0.63	0.88	1.24	1.97	2.96	3.77	3.41	2.71	1.28	1.68	0.68	0.71	21.92

soldier who was in the hospital with an injured wrist. When the ball and chains from his ankles were removed, he was so weak he could not stand without assistance. There were also several men who became ill from drinking black tea that had been adulterated with willow leaves. The lack of a privy for the hospital slowed a patient's recovery. According to a message from Doctor Knickerbocker,... "The want of this indispensable convenience has resulted in injury to the service to the extent of difficulties contracted by the sick and debilitated, when compelled to go through mud, rain and wind in search of such a retreat."

In addition to these problems the hospital's seven-acre garden was almost totally destroyed in 1869. The hospital steward and nurse discovered several cattle in the garden again. This time they returned to the fort for guns and ammunition and killed the two cows and injured a couple others.

A medical director from the army department inspected the post hospital on June 10, 1870, and released this information: "The condition of the building is such at this time to be totally unfit for proper care of the sick during winter season, for reason that the plastering is nearly off the ceilings below, and to a considerable extent in the attic—snow drifting through, under and between the shingles and ceiling."

During the 1880s, numerous changes were made to the hospital.
This view from the northwest shows the widow's walk on the roof.
State Historical Society of North Dakota.

Several repairs to the hospital in 1881 included new floors, partitions in the wards (with room for twelve beds), and new storm houses front and rear. The second floor was added and used as a dormitory for hospital attendants and a storage room.

The outside appearance was greatly improved with the addition of a fence around the hospital and a gravel road west of the building. Doctor James B. Ferguson, Post Surgeon, even planted flowers and rosebushes around the hospital.

Due to the dampness in the barracks, the soldiers were constantly ill. To combat this problem it was recommended that dried vegetables and salt, along with pickles, sauerkraut, molasses and tea be served at breakfast and supper.

Patients died from typhoid fever, smallpox, consumption (tuberculosis), pneumonia, scurvy and spinal meningitis. Since burials could not be made in the winter, a log house, sixteen by twenty-four feet was constructed in 1883 to house the dead bodies until spring. It was located south of the stable and was referred to as the Hospital Dead House. A 150-foot square plot of land directly west of the stable was set aside for the cemetery. It was enclosed by a picket fence in 1870.

John Other Day (Anoetu Tokeca). From an oil painting by Henry H. Cross.

Minnesota Historical Society.

John Other Day, a well known Indian leader, died at the fort hospital nine days after admission in October 1869. He had suffered from chronic bronchitis, and it was too far advanced to be successfully treated. John Other Day was a scout under General Sibley during the Minnesota Uprising. He was buried at the Ascension Presbyterian Church in Roberts County.

During the 1883 reconstruction of the hospital, stone masons had to stop to build a stone monument for the surveyors' work about a mile and a half from the post. Lieutenant Taber from the engineers unit cut a line on the monument and marked a point on the line, it being the starting line of the survey of the military reservation (a point in the center of the old flag staff and a point on that monument).

A new flag staff was put up directly west of the old post during July 1883. The old post was sawed off close to the ground and was left as a point of reference for the old survey of this fort when it was known as Fort Wadsworth, Dakota Territory.

During the same month the soldiers erected a carriage and wagon shed (135 feet long by 24 feet wide by 9 feet high), a few yards northeast of the stable. The ambulance, spring wagons and twenty-eight other wagons were housed there.

Men between the ages of sixteen and thirty-five were allowed to enlist in the army. A recruit had to pass a medical exam to enlist, but years later recruits also had to know how to read and write the English language. Those under twenty-one years of age had to have written consent from a parent, but soldiers sometimes lied about their age to join the army. A Mrs. Whitney from New York wrote that her son was a minor and that she wanted him out of the army. She was advised by the Commander at Fort Wadsworth to request a discharge from the Adjutant General in Washington, D.C. If his discharge was granted, he or his mother would probably have to refund the expenses incurred by the enlistment. The matter was dropped.

By the end of the Civil War, an enlisted man's monthly pay was increased from $13 to $16 a month. A new law adopted in May 1872 provided for an annual increase of $1.00 a month after the second year of service and for a bonus after the end of each enlistment.

The highest paid enlisted soldier was the chief musician who received $60 a month. A sergeant drew $17, while a sergeant-major and a quarter-master sergeant were paid $23 a month. Enlisted men also received clothing and equipment valued at $85 a year.

In 1866, soldiers working for more than ten consecutive days in the quartermaster, commissary or other departments were entitled to additional pay. Men employed as mechanics were paid an extra thirty-five cents per day, and laborers, an extra twenty cents a day. By 1884, this was raised to fifty cents per day for mechanics, artisans, and school teachers and thirty-five cents per day for clerks, teamsters, laborers and others.

The post office (the first in what is now Marshall County) was established at the trading post at Fort Wadsworth on September 14, 1865, with Jasper N. Searles serving as postmaster. The office was discontinued on July 7, 1873 but re-established July 8, 1875. During the time with no post office, the mail was carried to and from the Sisseton Agency by scouts. Two mail stations were established, one at the agency and the other at Buffalo Lake.

These three log structures appear to belong to the post sutler (post trader) located east of the barracks. (The area today would be between the road and the lake.) From left to right are the sutler's house, the store house and the trading post. It is difficult to determine exactly at which frontier post these buildings are from since they were built from local logs and look alike. According to Marvin Scott's *History of Fort Sisseton*, the von Minden sketches show three similar log buildings used by the post sutler.

Trading posts could be set up at a fort not located near a town. The post trader was a civilian who received his appointment from the Secretary of War and his license from the War Department. The trading post (sutlers's store) at Fort Wadsworth, east of the barracks, was a busy place.

In 1866-67, Major Brown was senior member of the trading post of Brown, Searles and Downie at Fort Wadsworth. Then, on November 5, 1870, T. W. Baldwin was appointed post trader by the Secretary of War; P. P. Shelton worked as a clerk with Baldwin until 1877.

An agreement, dated 1870, between Thomas W. Baldwin and P. P. Shelton stated that Shelton provided the money and Baldwin became post trader. Shelton, in turn, borrowed the money from the Simpsons and they (the Simpsons) were to hold the original deed as security. The Simpsons owned the oldest pawnshop in the country, in New York City, so one could say that the trading

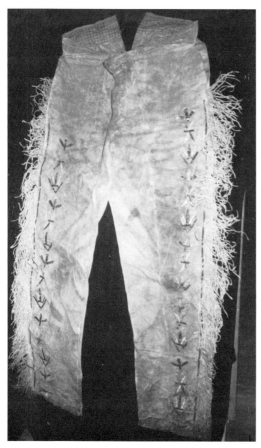

This leather trouser was purchased at the trading post at Fort Sisseton in 1881 by Martin L. Hanse. Red, yellow and blue dyed porcupine quills were used for the colorful design. Mr. Hanse lived by Hazelton Lake in Nutley Township. This is currently on display at the Courthouse Museum in Webster, South Dakota.

Johnson Photo Collection

post at Fort Wadsworth was once financed by a pawnshop in New York City.

In 1872 T. W. Baldwin was informed that his employee, George W. Spencer, brought liquor to the post. He was ordered to stop. The next month the Captain reminded the post trader he was not allowed to sell more than two glasses of beer to each enlisted man. If a violation happened again, beer sales would be stopped. Two days later sales stopped. Nine days later, Major J. E. Yard, recommended T. W. Baldwin as the proper person for an appointment for postmaster.

Then on January 16, 1873, the Commanding Officer ordered George W. Spencer to leave the military reservation within 24 hours and never to return. In 1877, Charles H. Handy was appointed post trader. Baldwin was again told not to sell liquor. By May, the Postmaster General in Washington, D.C., recommended Baldwin be relieved as postmaster and he appointed Miss Sarah Palmer in his place.

Numerous conflicts arose throughout the years regarding the sale of liquor. During those years, keg beer sold for ten cents a drink and whiskey for fifteen cents a drink or two for twenty-five cents.

In 1883, the post trader was using the room formerly designated as a clubroom for officers and their guests as a bedroom and office. He was ordered to clean up the place, as it was unfit for any lady to enter or even be near. The post surgeon was ordered to make an inspection and to report on the cleanliness of the store and corrals in his sanitary report.

On April 30, 1886, a tragedy occurred on the post when Charles Vander Horck, twenty-eight year old son of the post trader John Vander Horck, committed suicide. Charles was tending the trading post while his father John and his brother Max were in Berlin, Germany. Charles had slept late that morning, as he had been out hunting the day before and was tired. He woke up, ate breakfast and went back to bed. His wife went to the trading post and told them Charles was too tired to go to work. Upon her return, she heard a shot; Charles had killed himself with a pistol. Three months later on July 22, 1886, his father resigned as post trader.

Anna Abbot, the daughter of Fredrick Wilhelm Gustav Lindner, the post trader appointed in 1886 at Fort Sisseton, wrote the following article for the May 25, 1933 issue of the *Marshall County Journal:*

I recall many pleasant memories of my life at the fort and will try and give you something of the social life we had. You must remember that we were a comparatively small group, more like a large family of young people, living miles from a railway or others, not associated with military activities.

The officers' personnel consisted of major, captains, first lieutenants and second lieutenants, the persons holding these positions changed from time to time, but who ever they were, they formed the leadership in the social activities.

Two companies of cavalry stationed at the fort during the summers added much to the liveliness and picturesqueness of the fort. They camped in tents on the hillside south of the fort. Their Mounted Dress Parade was very interesting and entertaining.

Vacation time was always a lively time at the fort as children returned from college with their guests, spending much time horseback riding, swimming, boating and picnicking.

In the late summer and fall, activities centered around hunting. In this sport the ladies were as active as the men. Prairie chickens, grouse, quail, ducks and geese were the principal game of which there was an abundance. Game dinners were in order, of which we had many, and were always followed by a social evening.

In the fall with the young people returning to their various schools, the social life was more quiet until the holiday seasons, when they returned with skating parties, dancing parties and dinners.

The officers' club rooms were in a log house and did not have any of the modern conveniences of today. They were lighted with kerosene lamps, set in a trough, covered by green shades. Cards, billiards and pool tables were the winter pastimes for the officers.

The parade grounds, around which the buildings were built, was used for drill and parade, and it was interesting to watch, but the remoteness of the fort was such, that few outsiders were spectators.

While stories of deserters hardly fit into the story of the social life of the fort, the most exciting times were when news of a deserter spread and Jim King, the Indian scout, was sent after him with orders to bring him back "dead or alive." In one instance he brought the prisoner back across his saddle "dead", but after that he brought them back alive, the deserter knowing that when Jim King was sent after him he would come back and he would choose to return alive. Jim King still lives in the adjoining county of Roberts. He loved nothing better than to be sent on such a mission.

Like the homesteaders, the soldiers were always at the mercy of the weather. Blizzards usually created hardships for the men in the winter, but in July 1877, the weather was so hot that all the afternoon outdoor labor was performed between four and seven-thirty.

A violent windstorm caused considerable damage to the buildings on July 18, 1870. A northwest wind preceded by a blinding cloud of dust, gravel and rain at seven p.m. made it impossible to see even a hundred feet away. It carried with it everything moveable. The roof, rafters, garret, flooring and chimneys of company quarters were ripped off, and the walls and brick partitions were cracked. Later, most of this was found across the lake. Stoves were overturned, and fires were promptly extinguished. Only one man was injured.

The men from the north barracks moved to the quartermaster's building until repairs were made. Twenty feet of roofing was lost from the other barracks, which was covered with tarpaulins.

Captain John Vander Horck, 1830-1917. Captain Vander Horck commanded the troops at Fort Abercrombie, Dakota Territory, in 1862. He served as post trader at Fort Sisseton from 1877 to 1886. In 1885 he was one of the founders of Britton Land and Trust Company. The part of Highway #10 through the town of Britton is named Vander Horck Avenue.

South Dakota Game, Fish & Parks. Donated by Karl J. Vander Horck.

Three years later on July 29, 1873, another storm struck and damaged several buildings. Every window exposed to the storm was broken, and rain ruined the plaster in the buildings. Roofs were ripped off from several buildings. One hundred eighteen panes of glass from the hospital were broken. Even the garden produce was destroyed.

A sketch of Fort Sisseton as it appeared in the Northwest magazine in March 1886.
Minnesota Historical Society

Chapter Five

Keeping Peace on the Prairie

"I have the honor to enclose herewith "Special Post Returns"
of troops leaving this post discontinued this day. . ."
Captain Joseph Hale
June 1, 1889

Probably the most serious threat to peace on the Coteau des Prairies in the 1870s was the Drifting Goose Band. During the winter of 1878, Drifting Goose and his nomadic band of 200 followers drew supplies from Fort Thompson on the Crow Creek Reservation. During the summer they camped in an area east of the James River and drew supplies from the Sisseton Agency on the Sisseton-Wahpeton Reservation. Drifting Goose was a close friend of Chief Gabriel Renville.

Drifting Goose, Chief of the Hunkpati Band of Yanktonai Sioux, paid no attention to the government orders stating that he and his tribe were to stay on the Crow Creek Reservation. His band harassed and frightened settlers, surveyors and explorers, but never harmed them.

The following letter from Captain Bennett, Commander of Fort Sisseton to the United States District Attorney explains their situation at that time.

Headquarters Fort Sisseton, D. T.
June 15, 1879

High Campbell, Esq.
U. S. District Attorney
Fargo, D. T.

Dear Sir:

Drifting Goose's Band of Yanktonais Sioux Indians were born and have lived all their lives in the James River Valley on the James River, D. T. about 85 miles southwest of this post.

Drifting Goose and band attended the treaty at Fort Rice, D. T. in 1866 and declined to cede their lands, did not want to give their lands away by any treaty stipulation. Their fathers and ancestors had lived and died on this same land and they wanted to remain their with the bones and dust of the sacred dead. There was no white man's blood on their land. They had always been true devoted friends to the whites, had been allies of the whites and fought for us and with us during the Indian outbreaks and rendered valuable service to our people.

The Commissioners told them, so they say, and say it earnestly and give details, that they could go back to their lands and homes on the James River and there should live and in the peaceable possession of those lands they should be protected. Those lands should be set apart for their use and benefit forever. Treaty of 1866 to the terms of which I very respectfully invite your official consideration.

They joyfully left the treaty, the land was doubly theirs, it was theirs and continued undisputed occupancy for generations and what was theirs by right by lawful inheritance, was confirmed to them by this treaty. They went back and went to work to build themselves homes, and live as the white man did, because the white man so dictated. God only knows how those poor Indians toiled and lived year after year, almost without tools, implements or means to do with;their progress was astonishing, no one to aid or show them. They toiled on, the homes of their ancestors, honest peaceable industrious, they opened up farms, fenced fields, built houses and just began to see success before them.

Last year some white men saw those houses, fields, farms, cultivated lands, fences, gardens and wanted them. And from a letter from the U. S. Commissioner of Indian Affairs that was sent to me from James River Valley by a young fellow named Bingley—a letter addressed to Charles B. Foster (Same one that came to see you). I judge this is the way they went about getting those farms away from the Indians.

Certain white men went to those Indian farms and the Indians seeing whites trying to take possession of their houses, homes and lands, told them to get off their farms. They got off, then Foster reported to this Indian Commissioner that the Indians had driven him and his companions off from their farms (Foster and Co's Farms). Then the Indian Commissioner ordered these Indians to go to Crow Creek

Agency on the Missouri River. The Indians had a large amount of corn that they had raised on their farms. They packed up six hundred bushels and put in a pit in the ground, buried it and thus secured some other property, plows, Camp Kettles, Misc. Pans and Cups & c, & c and went to Crow Creek late in the fall as I understand intending to come back in the spring. Where they went, this Charles B. Foster and others, it is reported to me, went and "jumped" those Indian farms and took possession of their houses, farms, fields and some whites dug up and stole the Corn of those poor Indians.

One of these thieving white scoundrels, it is reported here, has run away and I understand the arrangement is to put the stealing of that six hundred bushels of corn on him but I am informed that there are other white thieves there yet.

I wish to ask you to bring this matter to the attention of the proper U. S. Civil authorities, that the facts in this matter may be got at and all the thieves engaged in this affair arrested and prosecuted to the fullest extent of the law. And I earnestly request that you will interest yourself in behalf of these Indians.

It is the strongest case of the Indians appealing to the white man for justice that has ever come under my observation. The whites owe a debt of gratitude to these Indians and owe them justice. And I sincerely trust the U. S. Civil authorities will prosecute and bring to justice all the offenders in this case.

I make this appeal to you in the interest of justice and humanity.

> I have the honor to be,
> Very Respectfully,
> Your Obedient Servant,
> [Signed] Clarence E. Bennett
> Captain 17th Infantry
> Commanding Post

On February 6, 1880, a portion of Drifting Goose's band came to the post to meet with Captain Bennett. The Captain requested First Lieutenant J. M. Burns and First Lieutenant George Ruhler of the 17th Infantry to be present at the conference in the quartermaster's office. Drifting Goose's brother (Santa-Yu-Ka), head soldier in the band, Ki-yu-kaupi (Standing Around), Shunka-Chis-Chells (Small Dog), Ka-hay-duta (Red Raven) and interpreter Louis Muller, half-breed Sioux, were present. They said they came to get their lands back, stating they waited all winter and at times nearly froze to death. They said they always obeyed the orders of the "Great White Father." Santa-Yu-Ka went on to say they were told to work the land; they had. They had been friendly to the whites and even helped them fight the hostile Indians during the Uprising. Some of their people were even killed.

Drifting Goose was not in attendance because he was in mourning for his son, who died. They asked for a place to stay for the night, some food to eat and some hay for the ponies.

The next day, they requested another meeting with the officers. They asked permission to go to Washington to confer with the secretary regarding their lands. They also presented the following statement which they wanted forwarded to the Secretary of the Interior for his consideration:

We belong to the SweatLip Tribe of Sioux Indians and from time immemorial our forefathers occupied a tract of land lying on the James River between Snake and Moccasin Creeks and extending as far east as Lake Kampeska. We have lived there since our births. Originally our fathers owned a much larger tract, but by degrees we have been concentrated on the land lying between the points named. We have always considered that land our home and that tract of land has never been ceded to the United States. We have built houses and fences on and cultivated that land, and we were making as rapid progress as circumstances would permit; when our homes were taken from us by the whites and we were left poor and desolate.

We had no shelter for our wives and children except our canvas tepees.

A little over a year ago, we were induced to go to the Crow Creek Agency on the Missouri River, with the understanding that we could return to our farms in the spring, but when we returned, we found white men in possession of them and they refused to give them up to us.

1st Lieutenant Burns of the Army, now at this post, was sent out there to our farms to prevent trouble. We appealed through him to the "Great Father" to redress our wrongs, he promised to forward all the facts in the case to the "Great Father". He advised us to go to the Crow Creek Agency and there await the reply of the "Great Father", we did as Lieutenant Burns advised and in July last we received the following order:

Executive Mansion
June 27, 1879

"It is hereby ordered that Townships 119, 120 and 121 North, of range 63 west, in the Territory of Dakota, be, and the same are hereby set apart as a reservation for the use of the Mag-a-badoes, or "Drifting Goose's band of Sioux Indians."

[Signed] R. B. Hayes, President.

In a letter dated February 7, 1880, to the Assistant Adjutant General in St. Paul, Minnesota, Captain Bennett stated that the orders of the President be obeyed. Seven months after the orders had been issued, the Indians still were

Drifting Goose
South Dakota Game, Fish & Parks

not on their lands. Bennett also said he had been informed that the Indians of Spotted Tail, Red Cloud and other agencies were watching with interest how the whites treated Drifting Goose and his band.

A month later Agent Colonel Crissy from the Sisseton Agency informed Captain Bennett that Acting Commissioner Brooks had decided the Drifting Goose case. They were to get two quarter sections of all the land. (C. B. Foster and Daniel P. Shilton were on those quarter sections). The tribe must homestead each and every claim, pay land office fees, occupy it and cultivate it for five years; they would get no title until the end of the five years. This must be done at their own expense without help or aid from the government.

However, two weeks later on March 17, 1880, Drifting Goose and two of his bands of Indians came to Fort Sisseton again to discuss the matter. They pointed out the Presidential Order setting aside three townships for them on their land on the James River.

In a letter to his superiors in St. Paul dated March 17, 1880, Captain Bennett reminded headquarters that there were between 25,000 to 30,000 Sioux Indians living within eight or ten day's ride of the James River Valley, many of whom sympathized with this band. He also stated that if Drifting Goose's band were to be removed by force to the reservation, it would be advisable to establish a military command in the James River Valley; moreover, vigilance should be used along the Missouri River to prevent Indians, west of the Missouri River from coming east.

On July 13, 1880, President Hayes revoked his order establishing the Drifting Goose Reservation, and the land was opened to settlers. A year later the chief was given permission to move his people to Fort Thompson on the Crow Creek Reservation. They went peacefully.

Drifting Goose died May 13, 1909, at the age of 88 and was buried at Stephan Mission Cemetery on the Crow Creek Reservation. He had been a chief of the Hunkpati Band for forty-five years.

Keeping peace on the prairie meant patrolling the area, keeping the fort operating, escorting beef herds to military posts, and providing military escorts for the wagon trains and others headed westward.

Commissioned officers and their men accompanied J. D. Skinner, engineer in charge of the St. Paul and Pacific Railroad survey crew in 1871. The party, under T. L. Rosset, returned in October that year from the Yellowstone River area in Montana, and as they stated, they had a "very successful expedition with thanks to the officers and men from Fort Wadsworth."

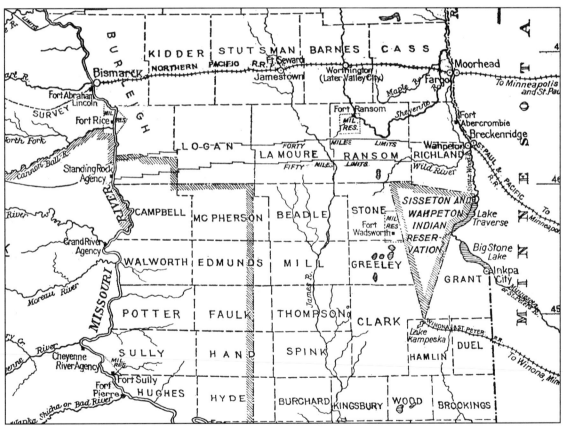

Part of Dakota Territory around 1876. The names and boundary lines of several counties changed within the next decade.

Captain J. C. Bates, 20th infantry, and forty-one men from Company B left Fort Wadsworth on August 31, 1871, to accompany the surveying party for the Northern Pacific Railroad from Fort Rice to the Yellowstone River on the Missouri. They put up a crossing on the James River and provided protection for the railroad crew.

On May 30, 1873, 20th Infantry First Lieutenant W. R. Maize, forty soldiers and two teamsters escorted the beef herd for the Yellowstone Expedition traveling from Fort Wadsworth to Fort Rice.

Twice, soldiers were called to the Ransom County area (now North Dakota) during the period from 1877 to 1879. An Indian scare that turned out to be a hoax brought some soldiers to the new settlement of Owega. Some settlers had reported seeing Indians in the Sand Hills area and a troop of soldiers was dispatched to Lisbon. As it turned out, the two Indian lads were just out hunting.

Keeping the trails in good repair was another one of the soldiers' responsibilities. Sergeant Schwartz was ordered to repair the mounds from Fort Abercrombie to Fort Wadsworth. The mounds marked the trail between the two forts. According to a letter from Captain J. S. McNaught, Schwartz was ordered to do the following:

...Each mound will be raised a full four (4) feet above the ground and the grass turned in where there are stakes in the mounds, you will allow them to remain, but where there are no stakes you will not be required to place new ones.

Ordinarily, the mounds should be one half (1/2) of a mile apart but they will in all cases be so placed that from anyone, two others (the one in advance and the one in rear) can be plainly and easily seen

You will send the spring wagon direct to this post from Fort Abercrombie, D. T. and will keep the Minnesota wagon for your own use...

Despite the fort's distance from civilization, it was sometimes involved in matters of national significance. President James A. Garfield died September 19, 1881, as the result of an assassin's bullet. Proper honors were accorded at Fort Sisseton on October 5. At dawn thirteen guns were fired, and this was repeated every thirty minutes between sunrise and sunset. At the close of the day there was a national salute of thirty-eight guns, one for each of the 38 states.

During the summer of 1882 about two hundred starving Indians came to the fort from the Indian Agency. Their rations at the Indian Agency had stopped June 30. After much consideration of the matter and upon examination by officers detailed, Commander Bennett deemed it absolutely necessary in the interest of peace and humanity to issue food from the United States subsistence stores to keep them from starving and scattering out among the defenseless settlers in search of food.

The Indians wanted to work and they offered to deliver one hundred cords of wood for five dollars a cord. They stated that they did not like to beg and expressed their gratitude for the food. Each family was given ten pounds of corn, four pounds of pork, two pounds of beans, three pounds of peas, one pound of hard bread, and a half pound salt.

Frank Roi, who assisted as interpreter, had a family of ten children and he was issued an additional five pounds of coffee and ten pounds of sugar.

The Indians stated that there was a great deal of favoritism shown by the Agency to Gabriel Renville, his relatives and friends. They claimed that six hundred cords of wood was purchased by the Military Agency, but the money went to Gabriel, and his relatives and friends, instead of to the Indians who had worked to deliver the wood.

The Indians were subsequently hired by the fort to haul freight in exchange for food and money. They hauled over seventeen thousand pounds of government supplies.

New technology reached the prairie fort in 1881 when a military telegraph line was constructed from the fort south to the Hastings and Dakota Railroad in Webster. Telegraphic services were provided to several buildings at the post.

There were thirty-two telegraph poles every mile, running a distance of 22.75 miles from the commanding officer's residence to the depot in Webster. The numbers from one to thirty-two were painted in large black numerals, each measuring six inches by one inch. These numbers were marked on the east side of each pole.

Captain Clarence E. Bennett.
Captain Bennett supervised most of the improvements made at Fort Sisseton.
South Dakota Game, Fish & Parks.
Donated by James and Lucile Muir.

Fort Sisseton, Dakota Territory 1883.

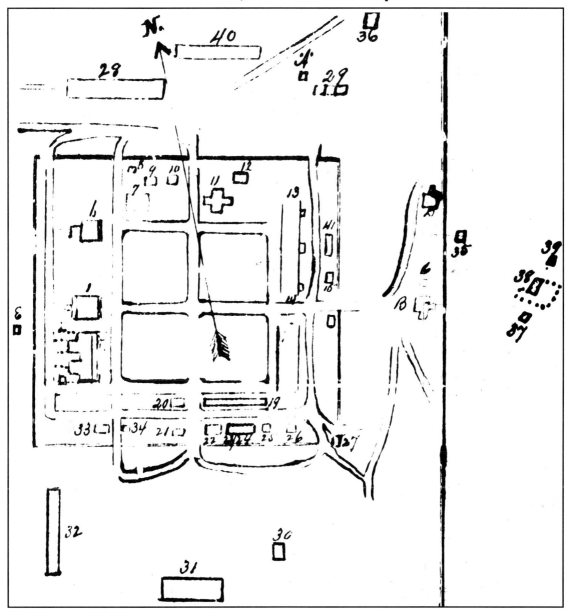

1. C. O. Quarters, 2. lst set Officer's Quarters, 3. 2nd Set Officer's Quarters, 4. 3rd Set Officer's Quarters, 5. 4th Set Officer's Quarters, 6. 5th Set Officer's Quarters, 7. Post Hospital, 8. Dead House, 9. Storehouse, 10. Log House (Scout's Qtrs.), 11. Library, 12. Log House (Laundress), 13. Co. Qtrs. Co. "I", 17th Inf., 14. Co. Qtrs. Co. "F", 17th Inf., 15. Post Bakery (frame), 16. Log House (Laundress), 17. Q. M. Storehouse & Office, stone 182 x 45, 18. Comsy Storehouse & Office, 19. Old Q. M. Storehouse, logs 150 x 24, 20. Office Comsy Officer (Adjutant Office), 21. Magazine, 22. Guard House, 23. Laundress Qtrs., 24. Laundress Qtrs, 76 x 21, 25. Laundress Qtrs. 32 x 26, 26. Laundress Qtrs., 20 x 30, 27. Saw Mill logs, 28. Q. M. Stable, stone, 29. Cav. & Blacksmith Shops, 30. Comsy Sergts. Qtrs., 31. Roof House, 32. Coal Shed, 33. Log House (Scout's Qtrs.), 18 x 16, 34. Log House (Scout's Qtrs.), 18 x 16, 35. Ice House (near lake) 24 x 45, 36. Ice House near B. Shop, 24 x 42, 37. Herder's Qtrs., log, 17 x 32, 38. Comsy Stable, Frame, 82 x 31, 39. Slaughter House, 15 x 15, log, 40. Wagon Shed, 41. Bath House, "A" Q. M. Platform Scales, "B" Trader's Store, "C" Log House, "D" Stable, "E" Old Log Stable.

National Archives Cartograph Branch Record Group 93.

Mile numbers were also painted on the poles. The painting of the numbers was done by E. C. Dampman, a musician from Company I, 17th Infantry. Both the pole numbers and the mile numbers could be read from a distance while driving or walking. If one became lost in a snowstorm, he could strike the telegraph line and know what his location was by referring to the numbers on the poles. These telegraph poles became definite landmarks during a storm.

The telegraph wires also needed to be secure because of storms. Captain Bennet reported in his own words how he personally saw to some of the wiring:

> Then I commenced to string the wire in a driving snowstorm, regular blizzard, November 2, [1881], and finished November 7, fastened wire to brackets on the roof and over the the window of the new depot building of the Hastings and Dakota Railroad, so it would be an easy matter to connect it with Telephone or Telegraph instrument in the telegraph office of that station; and at this end it is on a bracket on the porch of my office.

The work on the telegraph line was done by the members of the signal corps, who encountered a number of problems in constructing it. Finding enough good timber for telegraph poles created a problem since most of the best timber had already been cut and used. Indian Scout Sergeant James King (Akicitana) had four of his own horses which he rode while looking for poles. He rode one horse down and then took another and kept going. Eventually, they did find oak, ash, cottonwood, and willow trees to cut. However, many of the cottonwood and willow poles cut on the military reservation were not suitable for telegraph poles. Those were marked and later used for repairing cattle corrals and fence posts. Condemned oak poles were used to build houses for the guards and the cattle herders at the fort.

The men also encountered numerous other problems while searching for and cutting trees on the military reservation. Swarms of mosquitoes and numberous large grayish brown flies aggravated the men and animals day and night. The swarms of flying ants descended and continued to make life miserable. Several men contacted poison oak and ivy. Private Tribby chopped his foot with an ax. The men also stayed up one night fighting prairie fires, during which time twenty poles were lost.

About four hundred poles were cut on the military reservation before the soldiers got permission to cut on the Sisseton-Wahpeton Indian Reservation.

When they got the authority, the cutting was done under the direct supervision of Gabriel Renville and his interpreter. (Renville did not speak English).

The soldiers were often confronted with fighting natural disasters. On the evening of October 6, 1880, they spotted a prairie fire on the horizon. Winds blew directly towards the fort and carried sparks and burning particles over a fourth of a mile ahead of the flames through the tall, dry grasses.

The soldiers fought the fire all night while post trader Captain J. Vander Horck and his forces wet the ground around the woodpiles and haystacks. The laundresses also helped extinguish flames and sparks in and around the post. Fortunately, the government had supplied the post with Johnston Hand Force Pumps, which proved valuable.

Since 1882, the stage coach operated six days a week between Webster and Fort Sisseton. Leaving at seven in the morning, it arrived at twelve noon at the fort. It left the fort at one p.m. and arrived in Webster at 6 p.m. They took passengers, mail and freight according to W. M. Paul, Proprietor. A round trip ticket cost $3.50. The route was extended to Britton in 1884.

South Dakota Game, Fish and Parks.

Sometimes fighting the elements was just as dangerous as fighting a battle. When Hospital Steward August Gecks reenlisted at the post, he requested a twenty-eight day furlough with a recommendation for an extension of ten days. The furlough was granted. On Monday, March 19, 1882, Gecks left on the Webster mail wagon driven by Page Howe. The light spring wagon was drawn by two ponies.

The wind was blowing briskly, and there was moisture in the air when they left that Monday noon. The postmaster advised Howe not to start on the mail route because the wind had increased, and the barometer was falling. However, both Gecks and Howe wanted to go, even though they knew about the severity of Dakota storms.

Page Howe told Corporal Schin, Company F, 7th Infantry, that if the wind increased, he would take shelter at a house about five and a half miles from the fort until the storm subsided. About two-thirty that afternoon the wind increased, and it started snowing. The storm continued until about four or five o'clock, when it reached gale force. The storm raged on. Tuesday night Captain Bennett telephoned Webster and found that the two men had not reached their destination. He realized that they may have taken shelter where Howe had said they would. He also realized that Howe didn't always bring the mail directly back to the fort. He often took it from Webster to his home at Waubay before coming to the fort.

Because of the severity of the storm it was not a good policy to send out a search party. The storm raged on until Wednesday morning. Captain Bennett ordered a mounted search party to go to the house to see if they had taken shelter there. Lieutenant Edward Chynoweth and Sergeant Pederson's party consisted of three teams. Captain Bennett set out in his own horse-drawn cutter, following the mail wagon's buggy tracks from the post to the area opposite the house. At this time they found a place where both men had apparently gotten out of the buggy to look for the road. There were tracks to and from the buggy.

Sergeant Grib of the mounted party reported that Howe and Gecks had been to the house. It was apparent they had pushed on, thinking they would get to Waubay or Webster.

A scout followed the wagon track; Sergeant Grib was sent to the left, and Sergeant Redever was sent to the right along the telegraph line. Captain Bennett led the way to an area between the seventh and eighth miles. They noted that the wagon wheels were making straight clean cuts through the snow, showing the horses were walking along well. Bennett told Chynoweth to follow the track until he found the wagon and then return to Webster and report by telephone to him. Chynoweth found the wagon had been abandoned and continued to follow tracks along the sixteenth mile. At the fourth telegraph pole he found Gecks sitting, leaning against the pole, his feet and hands frozen and in an exhausted condition. At five o'clock he telephoned Captain Bennett to inform him that Dr. Harris of Webster was attending Gecks, but the doctor wanted Dr. Ferguson to come out from the fort.

Dr. Ferguson was ready to leave at nine p.m. on Thursday night. Sharp's team had been out, breaking the road for seven to eight miles. Details were sent out with lanterns and candles, and the remainder of the road to Webster was broken. But it was between five and six o'clock the next morning before they arrived in Webster.

A telegram from Dr. Ferguson to Captain Bennett stated that he planned on staying with Gecks for two or three days, if he had permission. Thus, Captain Bennett detailed himself to the duties of a Medical Officer. He also telephoned Lieutenant Chynoweth to continue the search for Page Howe.

Dr. Ferguson put Hospital Steward Gecks on a bed of hay in a government sleigh. Lieutenant Roach took another government team and drove in front of them for about six or seven miles to where they were to search for Howe. Bennett also sent out a breaking sleigh, that split the snow and packed it down, leaving a wide smooth path for the horses and mules to walk on. The doctor arrived at the fort with Gecks about three o'clock that afternoon. He was immediately placed in the hospital. Gecks told the doctor, "We pushed on towards Webster when the storm got so we could not see to avoid the drifts. The ponies could not pull the wagon through them."

Gecks wanted Howe to turn up the wagon. They had buffalo robes and blankets, an ax and a shovel. Gecks also had a large valise and a Saratoga trunk. They turned the wagon up with the trunk on one side, seats on the other and blankets and buffalo robes over them. They also placed clothing out of the trunk and valise under themselves. So situated, they could have gone through the storm unharmed. Then when the storm stopped, the parties would surely have rescued them. But Howe refused to stay at the wagon, according to Gecks. So each one took a pony. Howe took the best pony, but he could not ride him or even guide him. They were both probably frightened and did not know how to work together. Both ponies had bridles with which to guide them.

Gecks claimed Howe left him. Being alone, Gecks followed the telegraph line from pole to pole. They left the wagon between the ninth and tenth mile poles, and Gecks made it to the sixteenth mile pole.

Howe's tracks were followed to a house. The pony Howe rode was found dead near the house, and evidence showed that Howe had tried to break into the house, but failed. His tracks were found around the house. He had tried to break the door in, but the house or "shack" was fastened so securely that he failed to break in. Then he evidently tried to break into the house by prying the roof up, but failed again.

Citizens as well as those from the fort searched for the missing mail carrier. Page Howe's body and his pony were found three days later.

August Gecks was admitted to the Soldier's Home in Washington, D.C., on October 17, 1882. His discharge showed disability. His arms and legs were so badly frozen that they had to be amputated. The pony's back was frozen, but she survived.

According to the *Webster Reporter and Farmer* newspaper on February 4, 1892, the pony Gecks rode, 'Old Kit', had been purchased by M. P. Owen of Waubay from a band of Indians from the Pine Ridge Agency in 1878. Owen sold her to Page Howe to use on the mail route from Watertown to Fort Sisseton. Mr. Howe lived on the banks of Lake Kampeska near Watertown.

The Blizzard of 1888 in the Dakotas still ranks as one of the fiercest storms that ever hit this area. The storm lasted twelve to fifteen hours and vanished just as quickly as it started. The morning of Thursday, January 12, was warm and pleasant, and people spent time outdoors enjoying the unseasonable burst of warmth. This weather continued until mid-afternoon when everything suddenly changed. Temperatures dropped to thirty to forty degrees below zero and the fifty to seventy mile per hour winds whipped the snow and ice around.

Charles T. Davis, a stagecoach driver, left Webster with the mail enroute to Fort Sisseton. About seven miles from the post a severe blizzard set in. The wind was blowing directly in his face, and the storm was so severe that he turned his team around and sought out the house of a settler he had passed not ten minutes before. However, he was unable to find it. He detached his horses from the sleigh, set them loose and made a bed in the snow as best as he could with his buffalo robes and blanket. He turned the sleigh over, got under the sleigh and let the snow drift over it. Although the thermometer recorded thirty degrees below zero that night, he suffered very little from the cold. During the night, wolves came to the sleigh and fought over and ate a quarter of beef which Davis was hauling to the fort.

The next morning, he dug out, and finding that the storm had ceased, he took the mailbag and walked to the fort, getting in just before dark. While walking he froze his face, one hand and one foot slightly.

Afterwards, the men at the fort took up a collection of $40 and purchased a fur cap and a pair of gloves and presented them to Davis.

According to W. S. Horton, an artist who traveled through this area in 1885, the earthworks had been removed by that time, and the fort was a collection of buildings occupied by two companies of black soldiers and white officers. While Mr. Horton and his companies were pitching their tent near the fort, a soldier came over and said they could get straw for bedding; he also told them that they should get water from the fort because the water in the lakes was alkaline.

In 1885, homesteaders were moving into Dakota Territory at the rate of 5000 a day, claiming much of the land surrounding Fort Sisseton. The population of Day County had increased to the point that it was divided into two counties, Day and Marshall. Since the largest portion of the fort was located in the northern part, Fort Sisseton became a part of the newly formed Marshall County in 1885. Major F. Mears reported that the time had come to abandon the fort since the Indians were peaceful, and most were self-supporting.

Officers and their wives pose in front of the officers' quarters in 1886.
South Dakota Game, Fish & Parks. Donated by Karl. J. Vander Horck.

The lack of good water was becoming a problem in 1886. The men at the fort were forced to haul water eighteen miles round trip from Clear Lake. This was on the recommendation of Dr. Phillips because of the sickness caused by drinking the lake water.

A new well had been drilled in a vein of quicksand in February 1887, but with the lime and other solid materials it was deemed unfit for use, so they resumed hauling water, this time from Four Mile Lake and Nine Mile Lake. (These lakes, as well as Two Mile and Six Mile, still retain these names; they were named according to the distance from the fort.)

Even though life on the frontier was calmer by this time, the soldiers still had their duties, including marches. On May 9, 1887, the 5th Infantry with three officers and thirty-six enlisted men walked to nearby Buffalo Lake for a six-day practice march. Due to the lack of water, their route took them first to Nine Mile Lake, southeast to Clear Lake and Buffalo Lake, then back to Clear Lake and then due west to the fort. When Company G returned, Company E was sent out on the same route.

On May 23, 1888, Company E, 25th Infantry (black troops), commanded by Captain Bearle, departed for Fort Shaw, Dakota Territory. Then on May 30, 1888, thirty-nine members of Company G, 3rd Infantry, with Captain Hale in command, arrived from Fort Shaw to ready the fort for abandonment. On June 3, 1888, Company G, 25th Infantry (black troops), under the command of Captain Washington I. Sanborn, 25th Infantry, with First Lieutenant McMartin and forty-one soldiers left for Fort Keogh, Dakota Territory. Colored soldiers had been stationed at Fort Sisseton since 1884.

Excerpts from an article in the Marshall County Journal, Britton, South Dakota, gives us a glimpse of what the fort looked like at that time. P. R. Crothers of Badger, South Dakota recalled stopping at the fort in 1888.

...In the latter part of June 1888, my wife and I spent a night at the Fort while on our way driving through to North Dakota. At that time the fort was occupied by two companies of soldiers and a post trader and was a place of beauty. A large number of brick and stone buildings that would have done credit to any city were placed around the four sides of the parade ground. A fringe of trees skirted the parade ground on the south, west and north sides. On the east side were two very large stone buildings placed end to end. The north one with a porch along its west side was the soldiers' barracks and south building was the commissary. Along the south side was one fairly large building of stone and several small ones of stone and or brick used for shops, laundries, magazines and other purposes. Turning the corner on the west was a large two story brick building that was used for officers quarters and just north of that was a very fine brick residence that was occupied by the commanding officer. Around the corner on the north side was the brick hospital building and back of that and scattered along the north side were a number of small buildings used for shops, laundries, etc. Back of these small buildings and facing south was a very long narrow stone building used for a stable. About two hundred feet east of the two big stone buildings mentioned first were three log buildings, a trading post, residence and warehouse.

During the month of June 1888, no drills were carried out due to the amount of repair work the soldiers had to do. They finished building the oil storage building and tore down the old one. The porch of the officers' quarters had a new ceiling installed. The company barracks and the First Sergeant's room was refloored. The stable walls and coal shed were propped up to keep them from falling. The materials were there to repair the hospital, but there were no funds available to complete the task.

The post school for the children was still in operation, but there were no soldiers who wanted to take advantage of furthering their own education.

In July 1888, the Assistant Surgeon John L. Phillips reported a case of diphtheria and scarlet fever, both in the same patient, the post trader's child. In a Swedish settlement ten miles northeast of the fort there was a case of diphtheria. A child from that settlement had been brought in to the fort hospital for treatment, suffering from a severe form of the disease. The people who brought her were ordered to take the child immediately from the post, but her entrance to the fort most probably brought in the diphtheria. The scarlet fever, on the other hand, was undoubtedly brought in through the clothing of the relatives who were visiting the post trader's family.

Frequent patrols were still sent out, but the Indians were not causing any trouble. The homesteaders, however, were cutting timber and hay on the military reservation, and the patrols were doing their best to try to capture and punish them. Still, it seemed like a losing battle.

For several years, the post commanders had recommended that the post be abandoned since the area was thickly settled. In February 1889, a letter from the Adjutant General in Washington, D.C., recommended that Fort Sisseton be discontinued. On April 22, 1889, the Fort Sisseton Military Reservation was relinquished to the Department of the Interior.

During May 1889, soldiers prepared for the abandonment of the fort by gathering supplies to be sent to other forts. The last week in May they shipped 38,000 shingles to Fort Sully, 145 wooden telegraph poles to Custer Station in Montana and fifty wooden telegraph poles and 54 coils of telegraph wire to

Fort Abraham Lincoln in Dakota Territory. Two boxes of flags and signal canteens, etc.,went to Fort Snelling, Minnesota, and two boxes of other telegraph supplies went to Bismarck, Dakota Territory.

The official order was issued May 30, 1889, that the fort would be discontinued on June 1. Company G, Third Infantry, marched to Britton and then boarded the train to Fort Snelling, Minnesota. The fort furnished transportation for two officers and twenty-six enlisted men. The troops were inspected at 9 a.m., June 1, by Captain Hale. Privates Kelly and Washington of the Hospital Corps left for duty at Fort Shaw, Montana Territory. First Lieutenant McCoy and three soldiers were ordered to guard the post.

The last order in the medical book reads, "I have the honor to forward herewith the telegraph code furnished for use of the Post Commander."

[signed] Joseph Hale
Captain 3rd Infantry
Commanding Post

South Dakota Game, Fish & Parks

Chapter Six

From Abandonment to State Park

*"The establishment of the fort as a state park is one more step
in providing residents of this state and visitors with additional
tourist and recreational facilities."*
Governor Ralph Herseth
July 26, 1959

After the soldiers left Fort Sisseton on June 1, 1889, First Lieutenant
McCoy, Acting Assistant Surgeon David S. Swively, Hospital Steward John H.
Sanborn and Private John Green remained at the fort to gather up the miscellaneous items for an auction sale to be held June 6. Among the numerous
items auctioned off were 800 pounds of potatoes, stacks of lumber, a desk
from the commanding officer's residence, a street sprinkler and telegraph line
which had run from the fort to Webster.

Following the auction sale, First Lieutenant and Mrs. McCoy, their children
and servant and the three soldiers spent the weekend at the Commercial Hotel
in Webster. Then on Monday morning they boarded the train to Fort Snelling,
Minnesota.

The military reservation was turned over to the territorial government on June 9, 1889. First Lieutenant Frank B. McCoy, Third United States Infantry, turned the remaining fort complex consisting of twenty-two buildings over to E. R. Ruggles, the appointed custodian for the Interior Department.

Mr. Ruggles was the former telegraph operator at Webster. As an attorney he had served as Assistant Clerk of the House at the territorial capitol in Bismarck, Dakota Territory. Until this time, he and his family had resided on his homestead a half mile west of Webster. He moved his family to the fort on June 10, 1889.

This desk, from the commanding officer's residence, was purchased at the fort auction in June, 1889, by Fredrich Althoff. It was loaned to the fort and is on display in the north barracks.

Johnson Photo Collection

Almost immediately Mr. Ruggles started pasturing cattle and colts. He charged fifty cents a month for colts and a dollar twenty-five a head for the cattle. His herd of cattle soon numbered three hundred.

During his four-year tenure he used the fort as a site for social activities. Fourth of July celebrations became annual events, and dances were regularly scheduled. An intercounty dance held at the north barracks on February 23, 1890, featured lunch, basket socials and music by a five piece orchestra from Webster.

On October 1, 1890, Public Law Number 343, passed by the United States Congress and signed by President Benjamin Harrison, directed the land within the military reservation to be surveyed. In November 1891, W. K. Watson and a crew of eight men surveyed the remaining 81,000 acres of the reservation and divided it into quarter sections. The land was then turned over to the state of South Dakota. The state then sold or leased all of it except for the

The root cellar as it looked in the 1890s.

Chilson Photo Collection.

one square section of land with the buildings, which was to be used by the state for militia purposes.

Because the large block of land in the nearby Sisseton-Wahpeton Reservation blocked development of the surrounding area by white settlers, negotiations were begun with the Indians in 1889 for further cession of the reservation to the whites. In May 1889, a group of Watertown men led

The quartermaster's building as it looked in the 1890s.

Chilson Photo Collection.

by General H. R. Pease, met with tribal leaders at Big Coulee in Roberts County. This meeting resulted in a delegation's going to Washington, D.C., to sign a treaty (which became official March 6, 1891), opening one million acres of land to white settlers. This land was to be sold to settlers at $5 an acre.

On April 15, 1892, at twelve o'clock noon the Sisseton-Wahpeton Reservation was opened to homesteaders. Soldiers were stationed at each section and half-section line on every side of the reservation, their watches synchronized with the land office at Watertown, South Dakota. Their purpose was to keep order and not allow anyone to enter until the pistol shots were fired at twelve

The guardhouse as it looked in the 1890s. The ditch around the fort had been filled in before the soldiers left. It was later redug and resodded in the 1930s.

Chilson Photo Collection.

The barn in the 1890s.

Chilson Photo Collection.

noon. At that time each homesteader raced to claim his quarter section of land. Since soldiers were no longer stationed at Fort Sisseton, soldiers were ordered from Fort Yates, North Dakota, and Fort Snelling, Minnesota. Company H of the First South Dakota Infantry was ordered to be prepared to go but was not needed. Governor Mellette also ordered the sheriffs of Day, Grant, and Marshall counties to send a posse of one hundred men to help keep law and order.

E. R. Ruggles remained custodian until 1893 when Governor Charles N. Sheldon removed him and appointed Dan Hubbard to take charge of the buildings. Sheldon had promised Hubbard an appointment when he was first elected governor. At that time there were only twenty buildings on the grounds. Mr. Ruggles had torn down the two old log buildings and used them for fuel during the time he lived at the fort.

During the following years, people occupied the buildings for various periods of time. Some made their homes there while their homesteads were being completed. Others lived in the buildings while farming nearby land. A Mr. E. Russell wrote the following article for the *Marshall County Journal* newspaper:

...In 1896, I moved to the Fort to live while I was getting my claims ready to live on. The buildings were in very good preservation, also the walks and fences. The frame buildings had been torn down, sold and moved away by order of Governor Sheldon. Some of them were owned by private parties. There was a tunnel dug from the lake to the sawmill to furnish the mill with water. They used to tell many different tales about it. Some said it was dug as a means of escape should the fort fall into the hands of the Indians, but that could not be for it only went about half way to the fort...

Another man who lived at the fort until 1895 was August Rosenbush. He had first arrived at the fort on September 16, 1878, and spent the next five years there in the army. He then stayed on for six more years as a civilian employee. He worked as a mason, making his own bricks, and he built the oil house, coal storehouse, commissary sergeant's quarters and many other buildings.

Remains of the military and civilian personnel buried in the fort cemetery were removed and reburied in the Custer Battlefield Cemetery in Montana. (The name has since been changed to the Little Bighorn Battlefield National Cemetery). One group of bodies was moved in 1890 and the other group in 1896. A list of the burials is in the appendix. After the fort closed, early day residents buried family members in the fort cemetery. The graves are unmarked. Reburials from Forts Totten, Rice, Buford, Pembina and other frontier forts are also located there.

The hospital at Fort Sisseton around 1915.

South Dakota Game, Fish & Parks.

FORT SISSETON AS A RANCHING AND HUNTING PARADISE

During the early 1900s, the fort area was leased to the Fort Sisseton Stock Company. They used the hospital building for their ranch house and the south barracks for a barn. They set up a corral behind the two barracks. Mr. and Mrs. Tom Canton were in charge, and they lived in the building east of the hospital, the old library.

When the Fort Sisseton Stock Company dissolved, Herb Allen leased Fort Sisseton and the grazing land around it for twenty-five years. Cattle for pasturing were brought in from the three-state area. Andrew Gunderson was hired as foreman. Men were hired to repair the buildings, and major improvements to the hospital were completed and used for the Allens' summer home. The wooden sidewalk was in such poor condition that it was unsafe, so it was torn up. One of the barracks was used for tools and storage. The buildings were used year round except the ranch house (the former hospital), which was boarded up for the winter when the Allen family returned to Saint Paul, Minnesota.

During the early part of the century, many hunting clubs from the Midwest came to this area and rented area buildings during the hunting season. The Milwaukee Gun Club leased the commanding officer's residence for several years at the fort. Colonel William D. Boyce, a close friend of Herb Allen, leased the commanding officer's residence from the gun club during the summer. Colonel Boyce, owner of the *Chicago Tribune* and *Blade* newspapers, brought his family out here for summer vacations. His son, Ben, vice president of the W. D. Boyce Co., often spent the entire summers there, conducting his business by mail, listing his address as Eden, South Dakota.

W. D. Boyce, author, publisher and adventurer, spent much of his free time at Fort Sisseton during the early 1900s. Mr. Boyce is also known for starting the Boy Scouts of America.

Courtesy Boy Scouts of America.

Later, Colonel Boyce leased the hospital building for a year and then added a fireplace and converted it into a hunting lodge. The magazine was used as an ice house. Many stories have been told of the liquor brought in during those prohibition days and of the poker games that continued until the morning.

In 1912, Herb Allen and Colonel Boyce invited President Wilson and the Democratic legislators out to Fort Sisseton for duck hunting. President Wilson did not come, but forty legislators arrived and had a great time. Pictured above are some of the men and the result of their duck hunt.

Johnson Photo Collection.

Colonel Boyce, known as one of the men who started the Boy Scouts of America, invited friends here for duck hunting. Although Colonel Boyce brought his own personal staff, including cooks, maids, etc., many local people were hired as hunting guides, cook's helpers and kitchen help. Jerry Wilson of Sisseton was hired as the main hunting guide for Mr. Boyce's friends. Jerry was paid twenty-five dollars a day, a generous sum in those days. Other local hunters were hired to assist the guests. However, ducks were so plentiful in those days that even a novice hunter could aim, pull the trigger and bring down several ducks.

Hunter's Dinner
FORT SISSETON
SOUTH DAKOTA
SEASON 1927
MENU

Sauerkraut Juice

Olives   Celery

———

Cream of Tomato

Clear Green Turtle

———

Bass, Crappies, Perch and Northern Pike

———

Canvasback, Redhead, Mallard and Teal Duck

—Wild Rice—

———

Wild Goose—Wild Turkey

———

Grouse, Prairie Chicken, Pheasant in Season

—Wild Plum Jelly—

———

Asparagus Vinaigrette

———

Egg Plant   Green Peas   Baked Potatoes

Sweet Potatoes   Cabbage   Corn

———

Fruit Salad   Combination Salad

———

Ice Cream   Hunters' Cake   Fruits

———

Cheese and Crackers

———

Coffee   Tea   Milk

This menu was illustrated in color by Andre Bowles, an artist who spent several summers as a guest of Colonel Boyce at Fort Sisseton.

At one time, the St. Paul and Minneapolis Gun Club leased the commanding officer's residence. Herb Allen was founder and president of the club. Some of the members are pictured here in 1916 with their birds. Front row left to right: Fred Oliver, Dr. Theadore Mueller Jr., William Hamm Jr., Herbert Benz, Karl Houser Jr. and Louis Young. Back row: Otto Mueller Sr., Henry Pfeifer, Herb Allen, Charles Hauser Sr. and William Hamm Sr.

Johnson Photo Collection.

Guests took advantage of the putting greens set up on the lawn, the target shooting range using clay pigeons, the boating and fishing in the numerous lakes in the area and horseback rides to the Allen Ranches near Buffalo Lake and Waubay.

Guests lists at Fort Sisseton read like a Who's Who in America at that time. Among the guests were writers, politicians, jurists, physicians and business executives. J. D. Rockefeller, Jr., came, as well as George Balt, the manager of the Waldorf Astoria Hotel, and Senator Bartsfield from Pennsylvania. The presidents of Milwaukee Railroad and the Wells Fargo Company were guests here also. Furthermore, Gebhard Bohn of Bohn Refrigeration; Yoerg of Yoerg's Brewery; John Bradford and E. P. Allen, both lawyers; Herbert Bigelow of Brown and Bigelow; George Sommers, the wholesaler; and George Beckworth and Wm. Hamm of the Hamm Brewery were all seen here numerous times.

A newspaper article from the *Marshall County Journal* on October 30, 1913, titled, "Hunters Leave," adds more names to the list:

F. H. Welcome of the Union Investment Co. of Minneapolis; A. H. Poehler, grain commission merchant of Minneapolis; E. N. McGregor of Wichita, Kansas; A. S. Bennett of Renville, Minnesota; Dr. Hawkins of Granite Falls, Minnesota; W. O. Davis, paper pulp manufacturer of Neneah, Wisconsin.

During President Woodrow Wilson's term in office, Herb Allen and Colonel Boyce invited the President and the Democratic legislators from Washington, D.C., to Fort Sisseton for a hunting party. President Wilson couldn't come, but forty Congressmen came and had a memorable time. A private telephone had to be installed so the legislators could keep in touch and phone in their votes. The card-playing congressmen even brought their own dealer with them from their club in Washington, D.C.

In 1917, Herb Allen suffered a severe stroke and was in poor health until his death in 1921. His son, Herb Allen Jr., left Williams College and took over management of the fort ranch. To compensate for the financial losses suffered during his father's illness, Herb Allen Jr., started a new venture. He obtained a license to do commerical fishing and shipped out tons and tons of bullheads from nearby lakes to eastern markets. After his lease was up, he built a lodge on his land bordering the fort.

Colonel Boyce's death on June 11, 1929, brought an end to the hunting lodge at the fort. The Roaring Twenties had subsided, and the country was on the brink of a depression.

People from northeastern South Dakota were becoming aware of the necessity of saving the fort during the next few years. With the help of newspaper articles and local meetings, an organization was started to save Fort Sisseton. The American Legion Post Number 80 of Marshall County and the Dakota Lakes Association formed the Fort Sisseton Memorial Association in 1932. The following year the state legislature placed the Fort Sisseton land under a special board consisting of the Governor, Commissioner of School and Public Lands and the Adjutant General. The purpose was to sell or lease it to a corporation or group for the preservation of Fort Sisseton as a historical park. The result was the South Dakota Lakes Association, an organization formed in 1933 to preserve Fort Sisseton.

Fort Sisseton played a significant role in two Depression-era programs from 1934 to 1939, and these programs in turn aided in restoring the fort.

The south barracks as it looked in 1932.

South Dakota Game, Fish & Parks.

Under the Emergency Relief Administration (ERA), a federal program was set up to provide relief programs for states; as part of this program a transient camp, one of six in South Dakota, was set up at the fort in 1934. Between 125 and 150 men from a ten-county area were brought in and assigned the task of repairing the buildings. The original plan was to set up a dairy farm. Thus, the barn roof was changed from a flat roof to a gambrel-type for that purpose. However, the dairy barn idea apparently didn't materialize.

In 1935, another federal program, the Works Progress Administration (WPA), took over and the men continued the repairs, this time under the supervision of the National Park Service. To assure accuracy in the restoration of the buildings, the Park Service conducted a historical and archeological survey. The numerous artifacts unearthed in the digs were crated up and sent to the office in Omaha, Nebraska.

Hilman Rice of Sisseton was project superintendent from 1936 to 1939. The men (ages twenty to eighty) worked eight-hour days and then were on their own. The older men were given jobs like cleaning rooms and gardening, while the younger, stronger men were assigned the building and cementing jobs. According to the WPA records many of these men were paid forty dollars a month, with twenty-one dollars deducted for room and board. All of the men were responsible for their own laundry; the tubs, scrub boards and wringers were set up in a make-shift laundry room in their commissary.

During the 1930's, Fort Sisseton was one of the six transit camps in the state. Pictured above are some of the 200 men who lived and worked at Fort Sisseton. The men planted a 125 acre garden and had a herd of 60 milk cows. They were the labor force for repairing the fort during their stay.

Johnson Photo Collection.

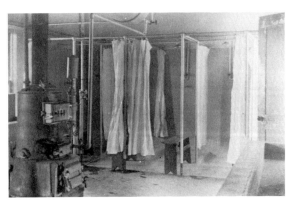

Showers were installed in the north part of the hospital for the men.

South Dakota Game, Fish & Parks.

When the men arrived, the buildings were in such poor shape that they couldn't even live in them. Twelve army tents, complete with stoves, were set up for the men until the buildings were made livable. Their bedding and kitchen equipment were trucked in from an abandoned camp in Wessington Springs, South Dakota. Army blankets were trucked in from Bismarck, North Dakota.

The men set up a commissary in the hospital, where they sold candy and tobacco and had a piano and a pool table. Barney Donahue was manager. Money earned was used to purchase milk cows from the government. Their herd of sixty cows supplied them with milk and cream. A bakery set up in the building east of the hospital furnished fresh bread and doughnuts daily. Although they had a 125-acre garden, other food

View of Fort Sisseton from the south after W.P.A. workers landscaped the area.
Courtesy of South Dakota Game, Fish & Parks.

supplies such as gas and coal were hauled in by ten trucks. Meat was purchased by halves and coal by the carload, most of it from Britton. Electricity was furnished by a light plant set up in the oil house east of the south barracks.

The blizzard in early spring of 1936 left the men blocked in for six weeks. By that time, their supplies of food and other items were dwindling, so Hilman Rice rode horseback cross country to Britton and ordered the roads opened. He ordered supplies, and within twelve hours, ten trucks arrived with much-needed supplies. Hilman rode one of the two race horses Dr. D. B. Rice stabled at the fort. Dr. Rice owned a race track at Britton and raised race horses. He had the contract as camp doctor and made regular calls as well as being on call.

At 9 p.m. on May 17, 1937, a tornado struck parts of Marshall and Day counties. The roof of the north barracks was lifted off and lay alongside the building, creating additional work for the men.

During the restoration days, several activities were held at the fort, allowing the area residents an opportunity to view the progress the men were making.

One of these events was the seventieth anniversary of Fort Sisseton, which was celebrated September 23, 1934, with a crowd of 7500 people on the grounds. The cold, rainy weather didn't dampen the crowd's appetite. The Relief Administration had furnished five young steers for a barbecue, and all of it was devoured by mid-afternoon. The festivities were sponsored by the American Legion Post of Marshall County.

Another public event at the fort was a tri-county picnic held on the fort grounds on October 4, 1936. It was sponsored by Day, Marshall and Roberts counties. The area residents noted the many improvements made. The earthworks had been redug and resodded on all four sides of the compound. The north barracks had been restored and was ready for the roof. The men had uncovered the foundation of the old icehouse on the bank of the lake east of the grounds. They had also discovered the bed of the engine and the saw used in the sawmill. The lake east of the fort, like many others in the area during the 1930s, was dry.

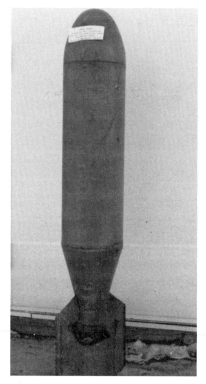

Furthermore, the Fourth of July celebration in 1937 drew a crowd of six thousand for picnicking, speeches, band music and visiting. Two years later, the Whipple Rodeo was the main attraction for a three-day celebration over the Fourth of July in 1939.

When the WPA project was terminated in 1939, the men were given rides to nearby towns and sent on their way to start a new life.

Fort Sisseton played a small role in World War II. In 1942, the United States War Department acquired 7,312 acres of land north, west and south of the fort grounds for an Air to Ground Range and a Low Altitude Bombing Range. This was in connection with the Watertown Satellite Air Field in Watertown, South Dakota.

About fifteen airmen from the Watertown Satellite Air Field (first known as the Watertown Satellite Airdome) were at first housed in Sisseton and then later at the fort. The last group of airmen lived in Britton, driving the eighteen miles

This is one of the sand-filled bomb shells the aviators from Watertown used on the bombing range at Fort Sisseton during World War II.

Johnson Photo Collection.

122

daily to the fort. Sergeant Nawassa was the commanding officer of the last nine men on duty.

Three observation towers were erected southwest of the fort buildings so observers could report the hits and misses on targets. The airmen also constructed mock airplanes set up on posts for target practice. These eight-foot-long "planes" had wingspans measuring thirty feet. Day and night, during the next two years, practices were conducted by the army trainee aviators from Watertown. They would fly their B-17's overhead and drop sand-filled "bombs" at the targets. (Another gunnery range was set up at Sieche Hollow during the same time).

One of these hundred-pound test bombs dropped by the B-17's was found by Alvin and Margaret Block and today may be seen at the Museum of Wildlife, Science and Industry on Highway 12, west of Webster, South Dakota. The bombing range operated from December 1942 until May 1944. In October

Blackhawk Drill Team. Otto Quade Renville, Post 50, Sisseton, South Dakota, often appeared at events at Fort Sisseton.

South Dakota Game, Fish & Parks.

1944, airmen removed the towers and other equipment they set up during those years.

The fort served other miscellaneous purposes as well during the 1940s. The Peppard Seed Company from Kansas City, Missouri, stored June grass seed and seed machinery in the south barracks. Public dances were held in the north barracks, and roller skaters also used the south barracks.

In 1947, the state treasurer transferred $25,000, the purchase price for Fort Sisseton, from the State Game, Fish and Parks Commission to a special military fund for the South Dakota National Guard. Then in 1954, the Fort Sisseton property was transferred from the State Adjutant General's Department to the Game, Fish and Parks Commission for a sum of $50,000 so that the fort could be maintained.

The National Horsemen Trail Riders, Inc., an organization formed for the preservation and restoration of the fort, leased Fort Sisseton from 1952 to 1958. They hired a caretaker, who lived in the adjutant's building.

Through the efforts of the Britton Lions Club headed by Bob Perry, and other organizations, steps were taken to designate Fort Sisseton as a state park. On March 2, 1959, Fort Sisseton became the eleventh state park in South Dakota. The dedication, sponsored by the Britton Lions Club, took place July 16, 1959. Governor Ralph Herseth and Will Robinson, state historian from Pierre delivered the messages.

Many special events celebrating parts of the fort's long history have taken place in the last few decades. The Dakota Territory Centennial Military Celebration was held on Sunday, July 9, 1961, and attracted nearly 25,000 people. Military displays included helicopters, the navy's Polaris, and the Air Force's Shark missile. On July 25 and 26, 1964, Fort Sisseton's Centennial brought out a crowd of over 20,000 people. In addition to the many speakers, the Indian pageant, the band concerts, the military parade and the jet aircraft demonstrations, a time capsule was placed in the ground by the flagpole. (The time capsule was actually sealed in the ground two weeks later). Items in the copper box are newspapers from the surrounding towns with accounts and photos of the activities during the two-day celebration). The capsule is to be opened in 2064.

The Northeast South Dakota Lake Region Association sponsored the re-enactment of Sam Brown's ride on Sunday, June 19, 1966. About twenty-five horseback riders retraced Sam's famous ride from Fort Wadsworth to the site of the scout camp on the Elm River and back again to the fort. The original

The visitor center in the north barracks, dedicated in 1968.

South Dakota Game, Fish & Parks.

150-mile ride a century ago lasted fifteen hours, while the re-enactment ride took place over a period of five days. Nearly one hundred riders took part during the last few miles into the fort. Basil Robertson of Sisseton portrayed Sam Brown. The program at the fort included state and national dignitaries.

Frank Farrar, South Dakota Attorney General, was the speaker at the dedication of the new Visitor Center in the north barracks on Sunday, June 30, 1968. Members of the Sisseton Legion Color Guard, called the Black Hawks, conducted the flag ceremony. The First Fort Ransom Cavalry Unit of thirty-five mounted men in full Civil War uniforms along with six army wagons, paraded through the grounds as the start of their eighty-nine mile ride back to Fort Ransom. (The five-day trip over military trails took them to Fort Ransom for their own 4th of July activities.)

The first annual Fort Sisseton Historical Festival and V. M. Starr Rendezvous was staged in 1978. Since that event, attendance at the annual celebration has gone beyond forty thousand for the two day festival. Held the first full weekend in June, the festival is now rated as one of the top one hundred

Fort Sisseton Military Reservation Markers

Bruce Semple and Ross Hinckley, both of Britton, stand by marker number 3. This post found in Section 20 of Wismer Township in Marshall County marked the northwest corner of the reservation. Bruce was farming this piece of land about seven and half miles east of Britton.

Chilson Photo Collection.

Floyd Johnson is shown by marker number 2. This post was found lying down at the edge of a slough on his farm. To photograph it, the post was propped up with stones. It marked the southwest corner of the military post in Liberty Township in Day County.

Chilson Photo Collection.

Frank Ringer stands by the marker in the northeast corner. Post number 4 was found on Frank's farm in DuMarce Township in Marshall County.

Chilson Photo Collection.

#3

#4

Fort Sisseton Military Reservation. Originally nine by fifteen miles covering 135 square miles. When the Sisseton-Wahpeton Indian Reservation was surveyed, a slice of the northeastern corner was removed, reducing the military reservation to 128 square miles.

#5

#2   #1

SW   SE

Norbert Janisch stands by marker number 5. This post was located in Lake Township, Marshall County on land that Norbert owned. This post marked the line where the Fort Sisseton Military Reservation and the Sisseton-Wahpeton Indian Reservation lines intersected.

Chilson Photo Collection.

Edbert Opitz by marker number 1. The post on the southeastern corner was found on land Edbert owned in Nutley Township in Day County.

Chilson Photo Collection.

A historic event for Fort Sisseton occurred in the fall of 1964, when Herman Chilson's research led him to the location of all five Fort Sisseton Military Reservation markers. The ten-foot solid cast iron posts were six inches square and bluish gray in color. About five feet of each post was visible above the ground. The posts were estimated to weigh about 1,200 pounds each— over a half ton. The raised lettering on the sides of the posts read, "Fort Sisseton Military Reservation, D.T." The tops were beveled with directional letters on three of the five posts.

The raised lettering on all the markers is the same and is still legible.

Johnson Photo Collection.

Fort Sisseton Centennial, July, 26, 1964. Governor Archie Gubbrud and other dignitaries were escorted to the stage by members of the Sisseton American Legion. The Commanding Officer's Residence is in the background.

events in the nation by the American Bus Association. The Rendezvous was named in honor of V. M. Starr, a nationally known blackpowder gunsmith and shotgun specialist who lived in the nearby Buffalo Lake area. Besides blackpowder shooting contests, there are military re-enactments, fur trading demonstrations, Indian dancers, and a military ball as well as numerous other attractions.

To commemorate the fort's 130th anniversary, a celebration was held on September 17, 1994. In addition to drills performed by the cavalry units from Aberdeen and Brookings, South Dakota, there were activities and programs for the visitors. New bronze information signs were installed in front of each of the buildings for the occasion.

Christmas Frontier is held the second Sunday afternoon in December. Outdoors, there are sleigh rides in the snow, and indoors, young and old par-

This stone feature, unearthed during the 1992 archaeological dig at Fort Sisseton, is a foundation from the bake house ovens. It was discovered behind the north barracks west of the bake house.

Johnson Photo Collection.

ticipate in making Christmas ornaments from corn husks, wallpaper, and cloth and join in stringing popcorn and cranberries. The final activities are lighting the candles on the Christmas tree and singing carols.

Archaeological excavations under the direction of Todd Kapler, archaeologist from the University of South Dakota, have given a glimpse into the past. During the renovation of the commanding officer's residence

The carpenter's, blacksmith's and wheelwright's shops are all under one roof.

South Dakota Game, Fish & Parks.

The Fort Sisseton Historical Festival attracts thousands of people each June.
South Dakota Game, Fish & Parks

in 1990, a salvage dig took place. Later, from 1992 to the present, digs have focused on the post bakery and the laundry sites. Thousands of artifacts (including bottles, nails, toys, and buttons and a host of other items) are visual reminders of the people who lived at the fort during the 1800s.

The Visitor Center and the Interpretive Center are set up in the north barracks. Several of the buildings are open to the public. Each year, more people are discovering historic Fort Sisseton and enjoying the peaceful, scenic setting. Extensive restoration plans are now possible with funding assistance from the Department of Transporation's enhancement program (ISTEA) and local fund raising projects.

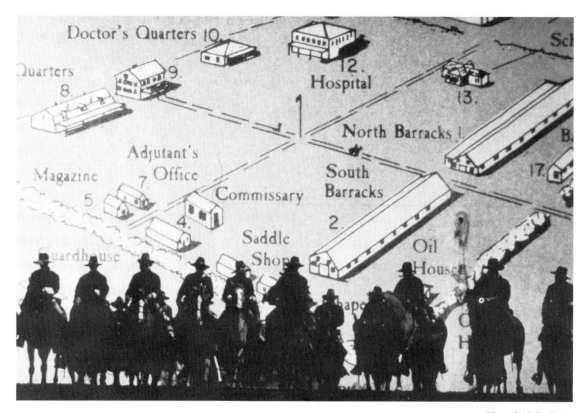

Doctor's Quarters 10

12.
Hospital

Quarters
8.

9.

13.

North Barracks 1.

B.

17.

Magazine
5.

Adjutant's
7 Office

Commissary

South
Barracks

4.

2.

Saddle
Shop

Oil
House

Guardhouse

ap

C
H

Photo by John Front

Today, Fort Sisseton State Historic Park is one of the few forts in the country with some of the original buildings on the grounds and it is one of the best-preserved forts in the Midwest. Built of bricks fired from clay along the Kettle Lakes and from the oak trees that line the nearby lakes, Fort Sisseton truly belongs to the land and to the people in the past, present and future.

APPENDIX

Commanders and Units
of
Fort Sisseton (Fort Wadsworth)
1864-1889

Assumed Command	Commander	Unit
1864	Major John Clowney	Wisc. & Minn. Volunteers
1864-66	Major Robert Rose	Minnesota Volunteers
11/64 - 9/65		Co. F., 1st US Volunteers (Galvanized Yankees)
1866 June	Capt. Peter B. Davey	Skeleton Force, MN Vol.
1866 July	Major S. B. Hayman	10th Inf., Reg. (238 men)
1868 July	Capt. William Stanley	" "
1868 Sept.	Capt. Hampson	" "
1868 Oct.	Capt. Thos. A. French	" "
1868 Nov.	Capt. I. R. E. Hampson	" "
1869 May	Capt. V. C. Bates	20th Infantry
1870 July	Capt. Joe Coe	" "
1870 Aug.	Capt. J. C. Bates	" "
1871 April	Capt. John S. McNaught	" "
1871 May	Lt. William Hawley	" "
1871 July	Capt. J. S. McNaught	" "
1871 Aug.	Capt. J. C. Bates	" "
1871 Sept.	Capt. J. S. McNaught	" "
1871 Oct.	Capt. J. C. Bates	" "
1872 April	Capt. J. S. McNaught	20th Infantry
1872 June	Major J. E. Yard	" "
1872 Aug.	Capt. J. S. McNaught	" "
1872 Oct.	Major J. E. Yard	" "

Date	Officer	Regiment
1872 Dec.	Capt. William Stanley (133 men)	" "
1873 Jan.	Major J. E. Yard	" "
1873 Feb.	Capt. William Stanley	" "
1873 March	Major J. E. Yard	" "
1873 Oct.	Major R. E. A. Crofton (129 men)	17th Infantry,
1874 Apr.	Capt. Malcomb McArthur	" "
1874 May	Capt. Edward D. Pearson	" "
1874 July	Major R. E. A. Crofton	" "
1874 Sept.	Capt. E. P Pearson	" "
1875 July	Lt. Col. W. D. Carlin (67 men)	" "
1875 Oct.	Capt. E. P. Pearson	" "
1876 June	Lt. S. M. O'Brien (60 men)	" "
1876 July	Capt. E. P. Pearson (59 men)	" "
1876 Aug. 29	Name changed to Fort Sisseton	
1876 Nov.	Major R. E. A. Crofton (55 men)	" "
1877 Oct.	Capt. John C. Patterson	20th Infantry
1877 Dec.	Capt. William M. Van Horne (43 men)	17th Infantry,
1878 July	Lt. J. M. Burns (49 men)	" "
1878 Aug.	Capt. W. M. Van Horne (49 men)	" "
1878 Oct.	Capt. C. E. Bennett (94 men)	" "
1878 Dec.	Capt. W. M. Van Horne	" "
1879 Feb.	Capt. C. E. Bennett	" "
1880 May	Capt. C. S. Roberts	" "
1880 June	Capt. C. E. Bennett	"1880 Nov.

	Lt. George Roach	" "
1880 Dec.	Capt. Clarence Bennett	" "
	(96 men)	
1882 Dec.	Lt. George Roach	" "
1883 Feb.	Capt. C. E. Bennett	" "
1883 May	Lt. George Roach	" "
1883 July	Capt. C. E. Bennett	" "
1884 May	2nd Lt. Edward Chynoweth	" "
1884 May	Capt. David Schooley	25th Infantry
1885 Jan.	Major Frederick Mears	" "
1886 Apr.	Capt. David Schooley	" "
1886 May	Major Frederick Mears	" "
	(92 men)	
1887 Sept.	Capt. David Schooley	" "
	(104 men)	
1888 Apr.	Capt. Washington I. Sanborn	" "
1888 June	Capt. Joseph Hale	3rd Infantry (39 men)
1889 June	Fort Sisseton Officially Closed	

Reburials at Little Bighorn National Cemetery
FORT SISSETON (WADSWORTH) — DAKOTA TERRITORY
1864-1889

No.	Name	Rank	Co.	Regiment	Date of Death	Cause of Death
1	Hiram Smith Benedict	Pvt.	C	2 Mn Cav	9-27-64	Fever
2	D. L. Maynard	Pvt.	C	2 Mc Cav	10-10-64	Unknown
3	James Gibbons	Pvt.	C	2 Mn Cav	10-18-64	Unknown
4	Benjamine F. Allee	Pvt.	C	2 Mn Cav	10-27-64	Typhoid Fever
5	Alvin Fredenburg	Pvt.	C	2 Mn Cav	10-31-64	Typhoid Fever
6	Hiram Harsh	Pvt.	C	2 Mn Cav	11-10-64	Typhoid Fever
7	Simeon Gifford	Pvt.	B	2 Mn Cav	11-23-64	Typhoid Fever
8	Henry Hollinshead	Pvt.	B	2 Mn Cav	12-03-64	Typhoid Fever
9	Peter Gulbrunson	Pvt.	B	2 Mn Cav	12-03-64	Scurvy
10	Frantee Saikora	Pvt.	C	2 Mn Cav	4-14-65	Bronchitis
11	Roy Anderson	Pvt.	B	2 Mn Cav	5-31-65	Drowned
12	William M. Coles	Pvt.	K	2 Mn Cav	12-07-65	Typhoid Fever
13	Lysander G. Harkness	Pvt.	A	2 Mn Cav	2-13-66	Frozen to Death
14	John Haggarty	Pvt.	K	10 US Inf.	8-16-66	Unknown
15	Daniel Hardigan	Pvt.	C	10 US Inf.	3-20-67	Consumption
16	Alfred C. Smith	Pvt.	E	10 US Inf.	7-28-67	Typhoid Fever
17	Peter Miller	Pvt.	K	10 US Inf.	2-23-68	Frozen
18	Thomas Flynn	Pvt.	C	10 US Inf.	2-25-68	Pneumonia
19	Rueben W. Russ	Pvt.		3 Mn Batt	11-1-64	Typhoid Fever
20	William Koch (Kock)	Pvt.	D	2 Mn Cav	8-24-68	Gun Shot/Fever
21	Lyman Buck	Pvt.	C	3 Ill Cav	8-30-65	Unknown
22	Louis Taylor, Surgeon				1-6-68	Gastrocide
23	Peter Tifferts	Pvt.	E	10 US Inf.	3-11-68	Pneumonia
24	T. Bradshaw	Pvt.	K	10 US Inf.	7-9-68	Bronchitis
25	Betty Rencer, Laundress			10 US Inf.	7-9-68	Consumption

26	William Condon	Pvt.	C	10 US Inf.	1-12-69	Inebriation
27	Philip McCarty	Pvt.	H	20 US Inf.	1-12-70	Inflammation of Brain
28	Louisa Roi, Laundress (daughter of Post Interpreter)				7-15-68	Consumption
29	Lieutenant Wood	Lt.	D	2 Mn Cav	11-25-64	Typhoid Fever
30	Francis Hubner	Cpl.	F	20 US Inf.	11-19-70	Drowned
31	George Rolfe		B	20 US Inf.	12-5-71	Frozen
32	Daniel Schultz		F	20 US Inf.	5-10-72	Spinal Meningitis
33	Wamatakanakau Indian Scout				7-20-72	Heat
34	Benjamin F. Brown	Pvt.	B	17 US Inf.	5-12-76	Gun Shot Wound While Deserting
35	Infant boy of Eliza Galloway, Hospital Matron	76 days old			11-20-78	Debility
36	Infant boy of Eliza Galloway, Hospital Matron	12 days old			1-11-80	Debility
37	Patrick Sheehan	Pvt.	I	17 US Inf.	12-23-83	Accidental suffocation while intoxicated
38	John Joye			17 US Inf.	7-16-83	Suicide by cutting wrist
39	Infant of Mary & Pat Schelling	6 days old			5-19-84	Debility
40	Unknown					Consumption
41	Unknown					Unknown
42	T.C. Brown	Pvt.	G	28 US Inf.	2-18-86	Unknown
43	Wife and Child of Pat Conrad				2-16-84	Unknown
44	Michael Duggan	Sgt.	G	17 US Inf.	5-7-86	Congestion of the lungs
45	Marshall Phillips	Pvt.	G	25 US Inf.	2-1-87	Unknown
46	Richard Pratt	Cpl.	G	25 US Inf.		Unknown
47	John A. Reed	Sgt.		7 US Cav	7-21-97	Unknown
48	George Taylor	Pvt.	G	25 US Inf.	10-21-85	Unknown
49	, Williams					Unknown
50	Unknown					Unknown

BIBLIOGRAPHY

BOOKS

A.B.C.F.M. *Sketches of the Dakota Mission.* New Haven, CN. Yale University.

Althoff, Simon. *108 Years in Dakota.* Privately Printed. n.d.

Andrist, Ralph K. *The Long Death,* New York: MacMillan Co., 1967.

Blackthunder, Johnson, O'Connor, Pronovost. *Ehanna Woyakapi.* Sisseton, SD Sisseton-Wahpeton Sioux Tribe 1975.

Bray, Edmund C. and Martha Coleman. *Joseph N. Nicolet on the Plains and Prairies.* St. Paul, MN: Minnesota Historical Society, 1976.

Buck, Daniel. *Indian Outbreaks.* Minneapolis: Ross and Haines, Inc., 1965.

Carley, Kenneth. *The Sioux Uprising of 1862.* St. Paul, MN: Minnesota Historical Society, 1961.

Chilson, Herman. *The Dakota Scouts.* Unpublished Manuscript.

Coffman, Edward M. *The Old Army, A Portrait of the American Army in Peacetime.* 1784-1898. New York: Oxford Press, 1986.

Department of Game, Fish and Parks. *Our Living Heritage.* Sisseton, SD: Courier Printing, 1979.

deTrobriand, Phillipe Regis. *Military Life in Dakota.* St. Paul, MN: Clarence Walworth Alvard Memorial Commission Publication, 1951.

Folwell, William Watts. *A History of Minnesota.* St. Paul, MN: Minnesota Historical Society, 1924.

Foner, J. D. *The United States Soldier Between Two Wars, Army Life and Reforms.* 1865-1889. New York: Humanities Press, 1970.

Hall, Grace Cynthia. *The Wadsworth Trail.* Morris, Minnesota, 1938.

Hickman, George. *History of Marshall County.* Britton, SD: Dakota Daylight, 1886.

Hurt, Wesley R. and Lass, William E. *Frontier Photographer Stanley J. Morrow's Dakota Years.* Vermillion, SD: University of South Dakota.

Johnson, Norma. *Wagon Wheels, Volume #II and #IV.* Sisseton, SD: Courier Publishing Co. 1982 and 1985.

Kapler, Todd. *Fort Sisseton: Report on the 1992 Archaelogical Excavations at a 19th Century Frontier Military Post in Marshall County, South Dakota.* Vermillion, SD: Universtiy of South Dakota, 1993.

Karolevitz, Robert E. Challenge, *The South Dakota Story.* Sioux Falls, SD: Sioux Printing Inc., 1975.

Leckie, William H. *The Buffalo Soldiers.* University of Oklahoma, 1967.

Marshall County Historical Society. Marshall County, SD Dallas, TX: Taylor Publishing Company, 1979.

Morris, H. S. *Historical Stories, Legends and Traditions.* Sisseton, SD: Sisseton Courier, nd.

Neubaurer, Project Superintendent. *Archaelogical Report,* Fort Sisseton, SD. Omaha, NB: US Department of Interior National Park Service, 1936.

Quaife, Milo M. *Army Life in Dakota.* Chicago, IL: Lakeside Press, 1941.

Quaife, Milo M. *Yellowstone Kelly.* New Haven, CN: Yale University Press, 1926.

Riggs, Stephen Return. *A Dakota-English Dictionary.* Washington, 1890.

Scott, Marvin. *The History of Fort Sisseton.* Pierre, SD: South Dakota State Historical Society.

Schumucker, Paul, Nohr and Associates, Consulting Engineers. *Fort Sisseton, Dakota Territory, 1888. Historical Review and Plan for Preservation and Restoration.* Mitchell, SD, 1974.

Sisseton Centennial Book Committee. *Across the Years.* Watertown, SD: Interstate Publishing Company, 1992.

Sisseton's 75th Anniversary Committee, *History of Sisseton-Wahpeton Indian Reservation.* Sisseton, SD: Sisseton Courier, 1967.

Smith, Sherry L. *The View From the Officers' Row; Army Perceptions of Western Indians.* Tucson, AZ: University of Arizona Press.

South Dakota Historical Collections. Volumes 8, 9, 15, 20, 31 and 36. Pierre, SD: South Dakota Historical Society.

Stallard, Patricia Y. *Glittering Misery.* Fort Collins, CO: The Old Army Press.

Utley, Robert M. *The Indian Frontier of the American West 1846-1890.* Albuquerque, NM: University of New Mexico.

Welty, Raymond Leo. *Studies in the Western Army Frontier (1860-1870).*

West, Nathaniel. *Ancestry, Life, Times of Hon. Henry H. Sibley.* St. Paul, MN: Pioneer Publishing Co., 1889.

White, Helen McCann. *Ho! For the Gold Fields.* St. Paul, MN: Minnesota Historical Society, 1966.

Woolworth, Alan. *Minnesota Indian Biographies.* Unpublished in Minnesota State Historical Society, St. Paul, MN.

ARTICLES

Allanson, George. "History of the Log House." September 4, 1931.

Allen, Don. "Drifting Goose Held Sway in Jim Valley." April 1970.

Chilson, Herman. "Early Happenings at Fort Wadsworth."

Grahn, Arch. "The Letters of John P. Williamson." The Minnesota Archaelogist. 1956.

Horton, W. S. "An Artist's Outing in Dakota." Northwest Magazine. March, 1886.

Renville Gabriel. "A Sioux Narrative of the Outbreak in 1862." Minnesota State Historial Collections.

South Dakota Legislative Research Council. Staff Report. May 27, 1958.

Stewart, Miller J. "Army Laundresses: Ladies of the 'Soap Suds Row'." Nebraska History. Winter, 1980.

Wright, Dana. "Military Trails in North Dakota, Fort Abercrombie to Fort Wadsworth, 1864." North Dakota History. April-July 1951.

Wright, Dana. "The Sibley Trail in North Dakota." North Dakota Historical Quarterly #1. April 1927.

BOOKLETS

Barrett, J. O. History of Traverse County. St. Paul, MN, 1881.

Chilson, Herman. Knickerbocker's 1869 List of the Birds of Fort Wadsworth Dakota Territory. Reporter and Farmer, Webster, SD, 1968.

Extract from United States Senate Document No. 23, 56th Congress 2nd Session.

First 50 Years. Dakota Presbytery to 1890 with Dakota Mission Past and Present, 1886. Reprinted 1984, Pine Hill Press. Freeman, SD.

Kandiyohi County Historical Society. The Great Sioux Uprising, 1962.

Minnesota Historical Society. History Along the Highways. Minnesota Historical Society. St. Paul, MN, 1967.

National Horsemen Trail Riders. Colorful Dakota Lake Region. Sisseton, SD Sisseton Courier 1953-4.

Neubauer, Franklin J. Project Supt. Archeological Report of Fort Sisseton. US Department of Interior. NPS Region II. Omaha, NB, August 1936.

South Dakota Game, Fish and Parks. Fort Sisseton Tour Guide. Pierre, SD Division of Parks and Recreation.

FROM THE NATIONAL ARCHIVES

Circular Order. Gen. J. M. Corse. December 2, 1865. NMRA

Commands RG. 98, Letters Sen No. 8. August 1875.

Department of Northwest Book 37, 66, 67 AGO

Fort Sisseton Letter Book 16, 1885.

Fort Wadsworth Circular Orders, 1865.

Fort Wadsworth Special Orders No. 156, 1867.

Medical History of Fort Sisseton (Wadsworth) Dakota Territory Vol. 1, Book 392. Group 94. Vol. 392, 395 and 397.

Quartermaster General Orders. RG 92.

Records Group 92 QMGO Person and Articles Hired. Fort Wadsworth, DT1226, 1191.

Records of the War Department, US Army Commands. Ft. Sisseton (Wadsworth) Group 98, Vol. 6-19, 29, 38, 39 ,40 and 41.

Senate Document Number 23, 56th Congress Second Session 1900-Material regarding Sioux War 1862, by Sam Brown.

War of the Rebellion Records.

NEWSPAPERS

Britton Journal 1942, 1946, 1959 and 1964.

Browns Valley (Minn.) Interlake Tribune 1931.

Grant County Review (Milbank) 1882.

Mankato (Minn.) Weekly Record 1865 and 1897.

Marshall County Journal (Britton, SD) 1864, 1865, 1913, 1933, 1934, 1960-1970 and 1972.

Reporter and Farmer (Webster, SD) 1886, 1889, 1926 and 1956.

St. Paul (Minn.) Pioneer Press 1864, 1865, 1866, 1873 and 1894.

Sisseton Courier 1917, 1937, 1942, 1958, 1967 and 1992.

Valley News (Minn.) 1966.

Watertown Public Opinion (SD) 1976 and 1979.

LIBRARIES

Ayer Collection, Newberry Library, Chicago, IL.

Beinecke Library. Yale University, New Haven, CN.

Congressional Library. Rare Book Room. Washington, DC.

Haye Institute. American Indian. New York City, NY.

MISCELLANEOUS

Sam Brown's map of Scout Camps.

Moses Armstrong Scrapbook MHS.

Original survey map in School and Public Lands Office, Pierre, SD.

Ralph C. Shearer's letter to Samuel J. Brown, Nov. 27, 1916.

Lewis Hill's Archaelogical Record MHS.

Microfilm #1179 of US Military Returns from Fort Wadsworth.

Other material derived from Herman Chilson's private collection and notes from the Joseph R. Brown papers and scrapbooks (purchased from the Brown family and donated to the Minnesota Historical Society), the Sam Brown diary and numerous personal interviews.

Interviews included: Gertrude Brown, Ed Crawford, William DeCoteau, Elmer Engebretson, Henry Hansmeier, Glen Hanson, Ludvig Langager, Vincent Malm, Alma One Road, Dr. Donald Parker, Will Robinson, Ovid Stevens and Helen White.

INDEX

Burton, L. S., 11, 51, 52

Camp Hagman, 34
Camp Lincoln, 6
Camp Ptan-sin-ta, 21
Camp Release, 5
Campbell, Colin, 31
Campbell, High, 92
Campbell, John L., 22, 38
Canton, Tom, 114
Caska, 35
Cayuga, ND., 27
Chamberlain Island, 21
Chappell, Darius D., 51
Chilson, Herman, 31, 48, 126
Chynoweth, Edward, 102, 103
Clark, Richard, 52
Clear Lake, 105, 106
Clowney, John, 1, 8, 9, 11, 12, 17,
    34, 49, 50, 51, 52
Cochrane, James, E., 42
Coles, William M., 63
Corse, John, M., 40, 58
Coteau des Prairies, 2, 8, 10, 12, 20,
    26, 27, 30, 35, 36, 39, 44, 45,
    53, 58, 60, 61, 62, 91
Courselle, William, 27
Crawford, Charles, 26, 32, 59
Crissy, Charles, 81
Crofton, R. E. A., 74
Crossman, 26
Crothers, F. R., 106
Crow Creek Agency, 94
Crow Creek Reservation, 91, 92, 94,
    95, 96
Custer Battlefield Cemetery, M. T.,
    113

Dampman, E. C., 100
Darrow, Jonathan, 38

Davey, Peter B., 54
Davis, Charles T., 104, 105
Davis, W. O., 118
Day County, SD., 21, 23, 53, 105,
    121, 122, 126
Deuel County, SD., 53
Devils Lake, 7, 8, 68
Dexter, Eugene, 63
Donahue, Barney, 120
Donnie, Mark, 50
Drifting Goose, 91, 92, 93, 94, 95,
    96
Dry Wood Lake, 60
Dumarce, Louis, 35

E-chana-ji-ka, 33, 34
Echat-tuke-ya, 13
Ecklund, A. M., 5
Elm River, 11, 31, 36
Emergency Relief Administration,
    119, 122
Eneehah, 13
Enemy Swim Lake, 10, 20, 23, 53

Farley, Dr. Charles I., 23
Farrar, Frank, 125
Feguson, Dr. James, 84, 103
Fertile, Charles, 30
Field, Albert R., 28, 29, 30, 63
First Fort Ransom Cavalry Unit, 125
Fisk, Andrew J., 29, 30, 31, 54, 55,
    60, 65, 77
Fisk, James, 9, 11, 12, 26, 60
Fisk, Robert, 26
Flat Mouth, Chief, 21
Fort Ambercrombe, 15, 28, 29, 35,
    42, 44, 47, 56, 58, 61, 63, 64,
    79, 97
Fort Buford, 113
Fort Hayes, 8

Standing Buffalo, 5
Standing Cloud, 22
Stanton, Edward M., 8
Starr, V. M., 125, 127
State Game, Fish and Parks
    Commission, 124
Sully, 6, 7, 60
Swively, David S., 109

Taber, 84
Terry, A. H., 26
Thompson, Thomas, 33, 39
Tomhpeyahote, David, 48
Tonkonxaiciye, 27
Traveling Hail, 5
Treaty of 1851, 2
Treaty of 1858, 2
Two Stars, Solomon, 13, 21, 22, 23,
    46, 76

Upper Sioux Agency, 2, 4, 5

Vander Horck, Charles, 88
Vander Horck, John, 88, 89, 101
Vander Horck, Max, 88
Vasseur, Francois, 18, 41, 42
Vasseur, Louis, 18
Virginia, Richmond, 58
V. M. Starr Rendezvous, 125, 127

Wadsworth, James W., 1, 12, 76
Wahhahchankah, 13
Wahpekutes, 2
Wah-su-ho-wastay, 13
Walker, Jim, 63
Walker, Philo, 30
Wa-mdi-u-pi-Da-ta (Scarlet Plume), 5,
    18, 19
Wanaton, 5
Waneta, Chief, 31

Warner, SD., 33
War of 1812, 5
Washington, D. C., 85, 87, 94, 107,
    111, 118
Wa-su-e-de-ya, 21
Watertown, SD., 24, 25, 104, 111,
    122, 123
Watertown Satellite Air Field, 122,
    123
Watson, W. K., 110
Waubay, SD., 102, 104, 117
Webster, SD., 22, 31, 98, 101, 102,
    104, 109, 110, 123
Webster, Viranus, 4
Welcome, F. H., 118
Wells, Mark, 34
Wessington Springs, SD., 120
Whetstone River, 53
Whitcomb, G. C., 29
White Banks Church, 47
White, Robert, 73
Wilcox, M. R., 43, 44
Wild Rice River, 28
Williamson, Rev. John P., 46
Williamson, Rev. Thomas P., 46
Wilson, Clara, 4
Wilson, James R., 27
Wilson, Jerry, 115
Wilson Mail Station, 27
Wilson, Pres. Woodrow, 115, 118
Works Progress Administration, 119,
    122

Yankton, 8
Yard, J. E., 35, 68, 87
Yellow Earth Creek, 10
Young, Louis, 117

Aerial view of Fort Sisseton in 1982.

ABOUT THE AUTHORS

Norma Johnson, a retired teacher, is also an author, historian and researcher. She was the co-author of *Ehanna Woyakapi*, was editor of *Across the Years* and was consultant for the *South Dakota* book in the *America the Beautiful* series. She wrote four of the programs for the South Dakota Adventures series for South Dakota Public Television. Norma wrote *Wagon Wheels*, a six volume set of books on local history. Her stories have appeared in several magazines and newspapers.

Norma was the recipient of the Dakota History Award, was selected to participate in the Oregon Trail seminar in Nebraska and the Stratford Hall seminar in Virginia. She was inducted into the Honored Women Educators of South Dakota Club in 1985.

During the summer months Norma works in the Visitor Center at Fort Sisseton. She and her husband reside near Eden, South Dakota.

Herman P. Chilson, a lifetime resident of Webster, South Dakota, acquired considerable stature in South Dakota and across the nation as a businessman, amateur historian, ornithologist, and book collector. He devoted over 60 years to extensive study, writing, and collecting which resulted in numerous publications. His expertise has been recognized at many levels, some of which included membership on the Augustana College Board of Regents and the Executive Council of the Minnesota Historical Society, recipient of the South Dakota Library Association's Friend of the Library Award, the Dakota History Confer-

Courtesy of Watertown Public Opinion

ence Award, and an honorary doctor's degree from the University of South Dakota.

A room designated "The Herman P. Chilson Collection" at the University of South Dakota is used exclusively for his private collection of over 20,000 volumes of rare and unique titles and many one of a kind resource volumes. Chilson's love of God, family, friends, nature, community, and country was exhibited in his numerous activities. His contributions in these areas will carry on in perpetuity and shall remain a point of thankfulness and pride for all who knew him.